T0360004

9781922800220

The Six Foot Track

Katoomba to Jenolan Caves

Updated 2nd Edition

By
Matt McClelland and the
Wildwalks Team

WOODSLANE
PRESS

in association with:

Australian
GEOGRAPHIC

Dedication

To the next generation, particularly Eric and Laura. I hope that we take great care of these natural places, and I trust that you can pass them onto your children, in even better health. Let's not settle for sustainability but work towards a flourishing environment.

Woodslane Press Pty Ltd
10 Apollo St, Warriewood, NSW 2102
Email: info@woodslane.com.au
Website: www.woodslanepress.com.au

First published in Australia in 2013 by Woodslane Press
This second edition published in Australia in 2018 by Woodslane Press
Reprinted 2020, updated and reprinted 2023

A catalogue record for this
book is available from the
National Library of Australia

Printed in Malaysia by Times Offset Printing International.
Designed by Kasun Senaratne and Jenny Cowan.

Contents

Note: Turn this book over for tracknotes running from Jenolan Caves to Katoomba.

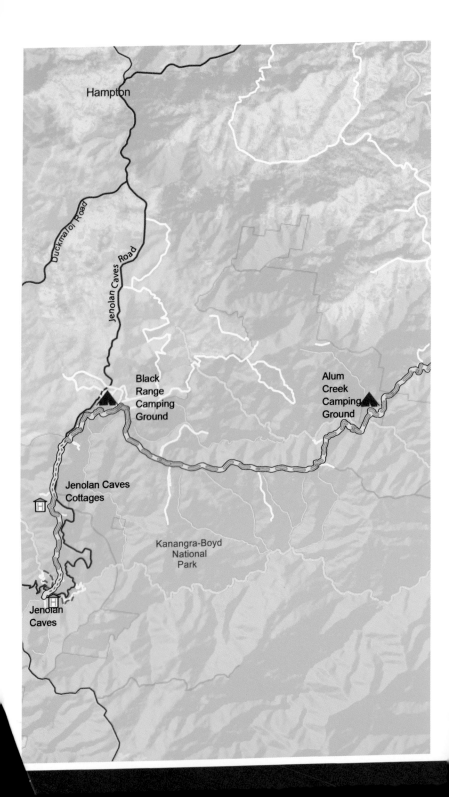

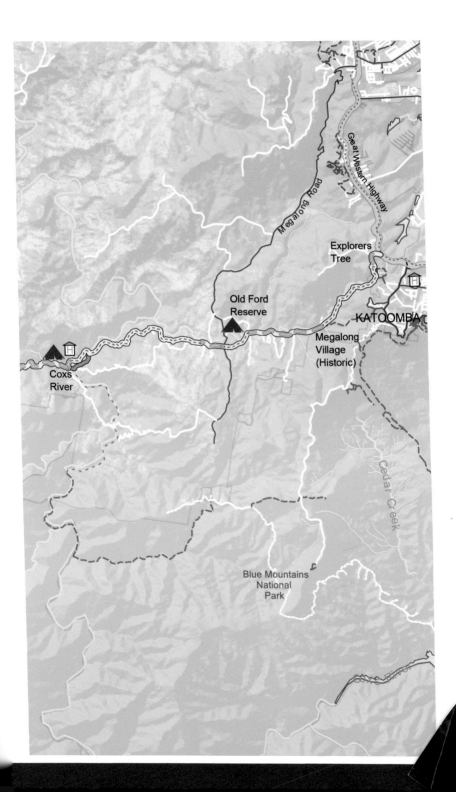

Introduction

The Six Foot Track is a not just a bushwalk but a historic journey – and a great adventure. Originally built about 2 metres wide, over 100 years ago, this route was quickly nicknamed the Six Foot (wide) Track. The name stuck, and now this walk takes you on a fantastic journey exploring the natural beauty and historic stories of this part of the Blue Mountains.

Starting from the Explorers Tree in Katoomba, the Six Foot Track was first established in 1884 to provide good access to Jenolan Caves by horse. Now revamped, this walk guides you through a mix of dense native bushland, past towering sandstone cliffs, granite creek beds, farmland, pine tree forests, and into the limestone valley of Jenolan.

Most people complete the Six Foot Track as a three-day hiking journey. The sense of achievement at the end of this historic walk is just fantastic, as is the chance to get away from it all and spend a few nights camping. You have the chance to share the track with a variety of Australian wildlife, such as wombats, kangaroos and wallabies, and a vast array of birds that you will see and hear along the way.

Whether you want to tackle the walk in one go, or split it into parts, this book provides notes and maps to help you plan your journey. You could try day walks, an overnight hike, an inn-to-inn luxury walk or join a tour group. The itineraries and information in the middle of the book will help you plan your walk at a pace that best suits you.

Introduction

As with our other books, this book is not just about helping you on track, but helping you get excited and organised for your walk. You may find the book also becomes a bit of a souvenir. Walking the Six Foot Track makes you a part of history – you will want to share your journey with other people for many years to come.

Acknowledgements – from Matt McClelland

First I would like to acknowledge the traditional custodians of the land the Six Foot Track travels through, the Gundungurra and Wiradjuri peoples, and pay my respect to their elders both past and present.

Thank you also to the hardworking people at the Six Foot Track Heritage Trust, Crown Lands, NPWS, State Forests, Jenolan Caves Reserve Trust, and to the private land owners. So many people and different organisations work together to maintain this track and the surrounding environments and allow us passage.

Thank you to Kieran and Ian who first documented the Six Foot Track on www.wildwalks.com.

Geoff Mallinson and Caro Ryan have worked hard to produce the companion website for the book, www.sixfoottrack.com. Their expertise

in design and video production has been a wonderful asset. Their friendship and willingness to help carry the huge load of batteries on track is still an encouragement to me – thank you.

To the people at Woodslane, thanks for your continued commitment to quality. Thanks to Veechi Stuart who had the vision and kindly embraced this unusual upside-down book. Thanks to Kate Rowe the most helpful and thoughtful editor, she helped make this book not only legible but enjoyable to read. Thanks to Kasun Senaratne for the wonderful design effort, the book looks fantastic. Kasun also helped design the housing for the 360-degree camera system I built to take more than 10 000 panoramic images on the companion website. To my family and family in-law, thank you for your support and love. To my wife Fiona who is so kind as to encourage and work with me. And of course, to our two wonderful kids, Eric and Laura, thanks for the joy and fun times walking in the bush.

How to use this book

This book has been written to help you get the most out of your journey on the Six Foot Track. It has been a lot of fun writing it and we are sure you will have a lot of fun walking with it. This is our first 'upside-down book' that allows you to choose which direction you want to walk the track. You can start walking from either Katoomba or Jenolan Caves and both directions are equally good. In fact some people do both in one go, over two days – this is called the Twelve Foot Track!

Introduction

The tracknotes have been written in a visual way to help you read through and get a sense of the journey. This helps you prepare for the walk and also helps you visualise the walk better, so you will hardly need to pull the book out whilst walking.

There are three main parts to the book: the tracknotes from Katoomba to Jenolan, the reverse notes from Jenolan to Katoomba and, in the middle of this book, lots of extra helpful information to help in your planning, such as the history of the track, best times to walk, itineraries, tips, safety information, and lots more.

Exploring the tracks around Jenolan Caves

Walk grades and times

Establishing grades and times can be a little tricky, and there are many ways to classify a walk. The walks were initially graded using the AS 2156.1-2001, Australia's standard for track classification. To keep things simple, however, in this book each walk is classified Easy, Medium or Hard.

Some general rules of thumb when looking at walk grades in this book:

Easy: Mostly flat, suitable for all ages and for people new to bushwalking; take care with children. Generally good track surfaces. No bushwalking experience required. May include gentle hills or short section of steps.

Medium: Suitable for most ages and fitness levels, especially people who walk occasionally. May contain short, steeper sections, with loose, rough or sandy ground, or lots of steps. Sturdy shoes recommended.

Hard: Suitable for people who bushwalk regularly. Contains steep or rough sections, and/or requires particular attention to safety, navigation and bushcraft skills. Requires reasonable levels of fitness. Sturdy footwear essential.

For the walk as a whole, a good level of fitness is required. You'll soon figure out whether your own pace is faster or slower than is shown in this book. The walk times do not include time for rests, side trips or safety margins; please always allow extra time. In addition, remember that hills can really slow things down. A relatively flat six-kilometre walk will take half the time of a similar length walk that climbs and descends 600 metres (Google "Naismith's rule" to learn more). This has been taken into account for all the times provided in this book.

Introduction

Preparation and safety

This is a guide book; it is not a field guide or a bushcraft book. You will find a few hints and tips in this book, and an extensive Safety section, but it is not designed to give you survival, navigation or bushcraft skills. Please read the information about safety, facilities and other resources carefully, and think about what food, equipment and clothing you will carry, and also where you are going to collect water, and how you will treat it. The notes will not prompt you to collect water, as your need will vary greatly according to the season, weather and your supplies. However, you must make sure that you have always enough with you to supply you on the next leg of your journey.

The Six Foot Track is a wonderful walk, but it does lead into remote areas and therefore requires skills and knowledge for dealing with hazards. All the walks have significant possible hazards, such as potential flooding, hot weather, lighting strikes, sickness, food poisoning, tick bites, falls, bites, strains, etc. Many of these hazards are not specifically mentioned in this book, and even though they are unlikely to occur each walker needs to consider and manage any potential risk. A bit of time thinking and planning will help you have a safer and more enjoyable time.

Introduction

No journey is risk free; but the better prepared you are, the safer and more fun your journey is likely to be. Do spend time getting your body and mind ready. If you are not an experienced walker, start by reading and chatting with other people and exploring some smaller, easier walks. The book has been written to help you prepare, but there is so much that we can't cover — you will need to think through food, fitness, equipment, risks and skills. If you do not have the skills required, invite a friend with the skills, join a walking club or a tour or group, or undertake a course; there are always people happy to help you learn.

Maps

The following symbols are used in the maps for this book:

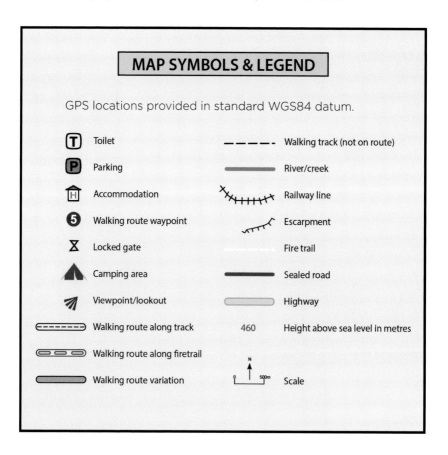

MAP SYMBOLS & LEGEND

GPS locations provided in standard WGS84 datum.

T	Toilet		Walking track (not on route)
P	Parking		River/creek
H	Accommodation		Railway line
5	Walking route waypoint		Escarpment
X	Locked gate		Fire trail
▲	Camping area		Sealed road
◢	Viewpoint/lookout		Highway
	Walking route along track	460	Height above sea level in metres
	Walking route along firetrail		
	Walking route variation	N ↑ 500m	Scale

1 Explorers Tree to Megalong Valley

This walk explores the most eastern section of the Six Foot Track. Starting from the historic Explorers Tree you may like to take a quick optional side trip to enjoy the wonderful views of Norths Lookout. The main track leads down the steep descent through Nellies Glen, through a lovely moist canyon environment with a few cascades. The track then mostly flattens out to explore some remote farmland and pockets of natural bushland. As you meet Megalong Road, there is an optional side trip down to a roadside campsite at Megalong Creek if an overnight stay here takes your fancy.

At a glance

Grade: Hard

Time: 3 hrs 15 mins

Distance: 8.2 km one way

Ascent/descent: 120 metres ascent / 600 metres descent

Conditions: The walk down through Nellies Glen is steep and can be slippery. There are a couple of creeks that can become impassable after heavy or prolonged rain.

GPS of start: -33.704, 150.2913

GPS of end: -33.7356, 150.2346

The shelter hut at the start of the walk

Getting there

Train: Catch the train to Katoomba station, and walk for just over 2.5 kilometres (see description below).

Car: Drive west along the Great Western Highway from Parke Street (the main road into Katoomba) for just over 2 kilometres then turn left into signposted Nellies Glen Road at the Explorers Tree. There is a dirt

parking area on the left about 60 metres from the highway.

If you are planning a day walk then you will need to organise a car shuffle or someone to pick you up at the end. From Blackheath, cross the train line then turn left to follow Station St, then right onto Shipley Rd, then left onto Megalong Road. Now drive along Megalong Road for just over 14 kilometres. Just shy of 500 metres after you cross Megalong Creek you will find a well-signposted parking area where the Six Foot Track crosses the road. (If the main road becomes dirt you have gone too far.)

Finding the track on foot from Katoomba Station:

From Katoomba Station head north-west along Bathurst Road (aka Main Street), keeping the train line on your right. Cross the roundabout, past the pub and a few backpacker lodges. About 1.4 kilometres after leaving the train station Bathurst Road sweeps right. Follow the road, then just past Narrow Neck Road (and just before the bridge over the Great Western Highway) veer left to follow the concrete footpath down the ramp to beside the highway. Keeping the highway on your right, follow the footpath over a siding and then take the short detour along the side road (Bathurst Road) before rejoining the highway again. After another 250 metres the footpath ends. Veer left, heading uphill along the narrow tarmac footpath (not the more obvious trail on the left). The footpath now zigzags up through the bush for a few hundred metres to come to the car park on Nellies Glen Road near Explorers Tree.

1 Explorers Tree To Megalong Valley

Point of interest – Explorers Tree (Katoomba)

In 1813, the explorers Gregory Blaxland, William Wentworth and William Lawson, on their historic crossing of the Blue Mountains, engraved their names not only into the history books, but also reportedly into this tree on the side of Pulpit Hill. The tree, now long dead, was caged in 1884 in an attempt to preserve the engravings. The engravings are no longer visible and there is even debate over the last 100+ years as to their authenticity.

Walk directions

1 From the Explorers Tree (at the intersection of Nellies Glen Road and the Great Western Highway), follow the *Six Foot Track – 200 metres* sign up along sealed Nellies Glen Road for just over 200 metres before veering left at another *Six Foot Track* sign. Here you will find another dirt car park and shelter with a large *Six Foot Track* information sign.

2 From the shelter, follow the *Six Foot Track* sign around the lower locked metal gate and walk downhill along the management trail. Continue down this trail, which becomes fairly steep in places, for about 500 metres where it flattens out and

comes to an intersection marked with a couple of *Six Foot Track* signs and a *Nellies Glen Bushland Restoration* sign.

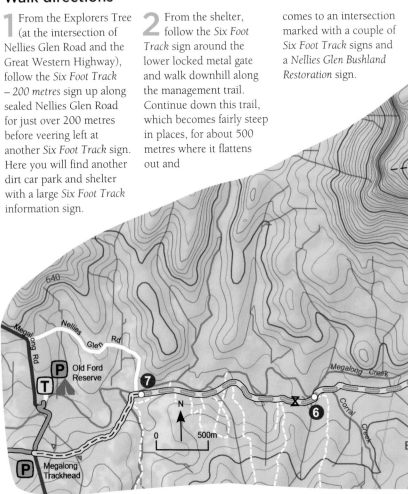

3 Turn right and follow the *Six Foot Track* sign downhill along the management trail past a few *Nellies Glen* signs as the trail narrows. After about 100 metres the track turns left and heads through green timber chicanes with *Caution – Steep Descent and Pedestrian Access only* signs. As these signs suggest, you now head steeply down through Nellies Glen canyon for about 300 metres,

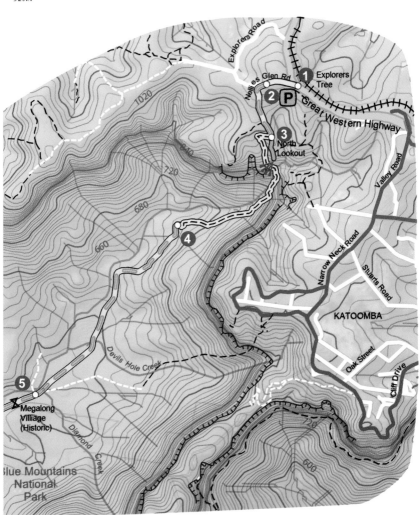

1 Explorers Tree To Megalong Valley

View from Norths Lookout

1 Explorers Tree To Megalong Valley

Walk variation – Side trip to Norths Lookout

From waypoint 3, continue straight on and walk through the gap in the large metal gate, over a small rise. The fairly narrow track soon leads down a series of timber steps, past some nice views for just shy of 150 metres to pass a faint intersection with a track (on your left), marked with a *Bonnie Doon Fauna Study* sign. Continue straight ahead, following the main track downhill for another 50 metres to the fenced and signposted Norths Lookout with great views over Nellies Glen and back over the valley you are just about to walk into. The lookout is named after John Britty North, also known as "the father of Katoomba" (1831-1917). North held large parcels of land in the area and was involved in oil shale and coal mining, running several firms including the Katoomba Coal Mine. North was also engaged with his community by sitting on several boards and local council and was an active member of his local church. Return to waypoint 3 by retracing your steps back to the Six Foot Track, then turn left.

down a lot of steps. You pass alongside tall rock walls and cross the usually small creek a few times before the track bends distinctly left to cross below a small set of falls. Here the track mostly flattens out and leads much more gently downhill along the side of the gully for another 400 metres to pass a *Blue Mountains National Park* sign. Just over 100 metres later you pass another sign marking the lower end of Nellies Glen. About 600 metres after this sign, the track bends to cross a narrow gully then leads up to a small clearing at the northern end of the wide Nellies Glen trail.

4 Veer left to follow the wide trail gently downhill. The trail leads generally downhill through the scribbly gum forest for about 1.4 kilometres to

then cross the culverted Devils Hole Creek – just past the creek is an unused concrete pipe with wild beehives inside. Continue along the trail for another 500 metres, passing an intersection with the Devils Hole Trail on your left. Keep heading straight here, following the *Six Foot Track* sign, and cross the culverted Diamond Creek which is a pleasant spot to cool down on a warm day. You will then pass the old Megalong Village site – now a horse paddock – on your left.

5 Continue straight ahead, walking past

Site of historic Megalong village

1 Explorers Tree To Megalong Valley

the paddock for just shy of 250 metres to head through a usually closed gate. Continue along the gently undulating trail for 500 metres, through the tall scribbly gum forest, crossing a usually small creek to pass a 40 km 6FT arrow post. About 400 metres further along this trail, soon after crossing the usually small Corral Creek, you will come to a T-intersection, marked with a *Six Foot Track* sign.

6 Veer right and walk along the Nellies Glen Road trail, keeping the powerlines to your right. After about 170 metres veer right at the locked Wari-Wari gate to climb the fence using a stile. Continue along Nellies Glen Road, which is now a public dirt road, for 900 metres, passing a series of driveways. You will then follow the powerlines again for 120 metres, passing just below a nearby house. Here the road leads downhill for 200 metres and passes a

Site of the historic Megalong Village

large *Road subject to flooding* sign. Just 100 metres after this, you will arrive at an intersection with a *Six Foot Track* sign and stile, just before the road bends right to cross Megalong Creek at a pleasant ford.

7 Unless you would like to check out the creek, continue straight ahead, following the *Six Foot Track* sign by climbing over the fence using the stile. A sign reminds walkers to stay on the track as this section is on private property. Walk through the mostly open farmland for 130 metres,

passing a *Private Land No Camping sign*. You will then cross Mitchells Creek – this creek may become impassable after heavy or prolonged rain.

Over the next 300 metres the trail leads over a rise through the open farmland, with a nice view of the escarpment behind you. You then cross a fence using a stile on your right, and continue through denser forest for another 300 metres to cross Mclennan Bridge, named after Mr Michael (Mick) Mclellan who has been in

charge of maintaining the Six Foot Track for many years. Just shy of 150 metres after the bridge, continue straight at a four-way intersection, then after 200 metres climb over another fence using a stile. Here you will cross the sealed Megalong Road, to find a car park beside a clearing and several Six *Foot Track* signposts.

(To continue along the Six Foot Track, head straight on, following the notes in the next walk: **Megalong Valley to Coxs River Campsite**.)

Megalong Creek at Old Ford Reserve

Walk variation – Alternate route to Old Ford Reserve campsite

From the end of this walk, at the Megalong Trackhead, turn right to follow the *Old Ford Reserve Picnic & Camping Ground 500 metres* sign gently downhill along sealed Megalong Road. After about 360 metres the road bends left then leads down to cross Megalong Creek on the raised concrete ford — this creek does flood at times and can become unsafe to cross. Just after crossing the creek, veer right into the large car-based camping area. Old Ford Reserve campsite is on the northern bank of Megalong Creek. The campsite is accessible by car, has a wheelchair-accessible toilet, and plenty of flat space to pitch a tent. You may spot a wombat or eastern grey kangaroo here and the nice groupings of trees and access to the creek make this a pleasant enough place to stay. Being on the side of the road this campsite does attract some loud campers at times.

2 Megalong Valley to Coxs River Campsite

This section of the Six Foot Track explores a mix of farmland and native forest before giving you the opportunity to explore the beautiful Coxs River. Starting with a touch of history at the old Megalong Cemetery, you then wander through open farmland with some great views back to the distant escarpment. Behind the farms you continue through a few pleasant valleys and down the side of the valley to the granite edges of the Coxs River. After some time cooling off, you can choose to wade through the river, or bring out your inner adventurer on the memorable Bowtells metal swing bridge above. The dirt road at the end of this walk is 4WD access only from Jenolan Caves Rd.

At a glance

Grade: Medium

Time: 3 hrs

Distance: 7.5 km one way

Ascent/descent: 310 metres ascent/610 metres descent

Conditions: All the significant waterway crossings are bridged. Best to avoid on very hot days, although on warm days you can make the most of the Coxs River.

GPS of start: -33.7356, 150.2346
GPS of end: -33.7433, 150.1787

Bowtells Bridge

2 Megalong Valley to Coxs River Campsite

Getting there

Car: From Blackheath, cross the train line, turn left to follow Station Street then right onto Shipley Road and left onto Megalong Road. Now drive along Megalong Road for just over 14 kilometres. Soon after you cross Megalong Creek you will find a well-signposted parking area where the Six Foot Track crosses the road. (If the main road becomes dirt you have gone too far.)

Driving to the Coxs River Campsite: If doing this as a day walk, it will usually be easier to allow extra time and retrace your steps back to the start, but car access is possible in a 4WD to the Coxs River Campsite. Follow the driving directions, then the tracknotes for the Black Range campsite to Coxs River walk (turn this book over, and go to page 17), as that walk follows the road all the way. At times this can be a challenging drive and some four wheel driving experience is recommended.

Walk directions

1 From the car park on Megalong Road (about 400 metres south of Megalong Creek), follow the *Six Foot Track* sign over the cattle grid or stile and check out the large sheltered *Six Foot Track* information sign. Now continue gently downhill along the dirt road (away from Megalong Road) for about 80 metres to arrive beside a stone memorial, marking Megalong Cemetery on your left.

2 Continue straight ahead for about 80 metres, still heading downhill along the dirt road, and pass through a gate with a *No Through Road sign*. About 300 metres later you pass a few driveways, beside the farmland, and cross another cattle grid. Then after another 150 metres the road leads you close to Megalong Creek, where a sign reminds

Point of interest – Megalong Cemetery

The Megalong Cemetery became the final resting place for at least 14 people who died between 1894 and 1931. It is very overgrown, and many of the grave sites are in poor repair or can no longer be easily found – please take care in the area to avoid any further damage. A tall stone monument marks the edge of the cemetery. This cemetery is currently under the management of the Blue Mountains City Council, and is recognised by the National Trust.

visitors this is private land. About 30 metres further on, stay on the main dirt road as it veers right at a Y-intersection, then cross a cattle grid. Now wander uphill, still on the dirt road, for just over 200 metres, with views of the escarpment behind you, to cross another grid and come to an intersection marked with a *Six Foot Track* sign.

3 Turn right to follow the *Six Foot Track* sign downhill along the narrow track into the valley. Cross a small creek on the timber Guyver Bridge, named in honour of Jon Guyver who worked hard to redevelop the Six Foot Track as the track coordinator/ administrator until 2010. Head up a series of timber steps and over a rise. The track now leads you alongside a wire fence for almost 100 metres, down through the farmland and across a valley above a dam, to a metal stile just before a dirt driveway. Turn right here and climb the fence using the stile, then follow the *Six Foot Track* sign. The track undulates over a series of hills for about 300 metres before crossing another fence using another metal stile beside a large tree. Stay on the track as it leads you uphill for 200 metres to pass a *Private Land – No Camping before Coxs River Reserve* sign, then meander along the side of the hill

for a further 150 metres before heading into a wooded forest and down some timber steps. Cross a steep gully and continue along the side of this hill for just over 100 metres, passing a *35 km 6FT* arrow post, then 150 metres later cross another fence using a metal stile. Continue for 600 metres through a mix of farmland and open forest, crossing a few more steep gullies with timber steps. Then you will head through a gate (make sure to close it behind you), marked with a few *Private Property* signs.

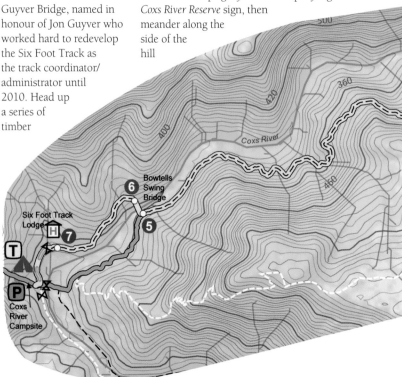

4 Continue walking downhill along the narrowing track, keeping the Coxs River Valley to your right. After about 120 metres, cross a timber fence on a metal stile, then continue down the track over a few large rocks for just over 200 metres to an intersection with a wide trail. Follow the signs and turn right then immediately left and continue along the track as it narrows again. The track continues down along the side

of the valley for about 600 metres and passes through another usually closed gate. After another 250 metres, the track leads you past a few pleasant granite boulders then down a few timber steps. About 400 metres after this, you walk down a 100-metre-long series of timber steps to cross a gully. Here there is a series of large granite boulders, and one of the small overhangs is

home to a wild beehive, which is worth checking out. The track now leads you out of this gully and continues more gently down along the side of the hill for about one kilometre, where the valley opens up with wider views to the Coxs River. Head down two sets of timber steps with a 250-metre gap in between, then walk through a pleasant lush gully with

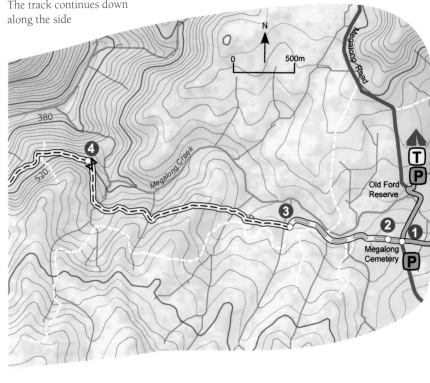

Australian fauna – Wombats

You are fairly likely to meet a wombat or at least see some of their burrows whilst walking the Six Foot Track. They are incredible creatures unique to Australia. Wombats use their claws and teeth to dig complex, sizable burrows as their homes. They even have backward-facing pouches that keep the babies warm and safe from dirt while tunnelling. Keep an eye out for the cube-shaped scat near the entrance to their burrows. Wombats will leave nearly 100 dry cubic poos around their burrow each night – we don't really how they end up cube-shaped! The diprotodon, a long extinct, distant relative of the wombat, once roamed these forests – think "two-metre-tall rhinoceros-like wombat" and you'll have a pretty good picture of the diprotodon!

views close to the nearby river – keep a lookout for willy wagtails between the casuarinas here. In another 150 metres you will find an intersection just above the swing bridge, to your right, marked with a *Six Foot Track* and *Alternative Bridge* signs.

5 Turn right and follow the *Alternative Bridge When River High* sign down the timber steps to the southern end of the Bowtells Bridge. (For more about the history of this bridge, see page 30.) Here you can scramble down the large granite boulders to play at the river, but be aware that these rocks can get very slippery. When you are ready to cross,

Walk variation – Alternate route to the Coxs River Campsite

From waypoint 5, continue straight ahead, passing just above Bowtells Swing Bridge, and following the Six Foot Track sign along the clear track with the main valley to your right. After about 30 metres you will pass an intersection with another track (which leads to the bridge), then continue along the side of the hill for about 800 metres. You will cross several gullies and arrive at an intersection with a wide trail beside a short timber fence. Continue beside this fence for about 70 metres then turn right to follow the Six Foot Track sign steeply down the embankment. Now follow the faint track across the open floodplain to the bank of the Coxs River. If conditions are favourable find a good place and cross the river. The river may flow in two or three sections across smooth and slippery rocks, or you can cross in the deeper sandy section. This river becomes impassable when in flood, but is normally only shin-deep in the rocky section – if deeper or moving fast, consider using the swing bridge upstream. Once on the sandy beach on the far side, follow the wide trail uphill for about 40 metres, passing around the metal gate, and find the intersection marked with a *Six Foot Track* sign. The Coxs River Campsite is just on the other side of the dirt road up to your right.

climb the ramp and walk high above the Coxs River on the suspension bridge, observing the *Only one Person at a time* safety sign. This crossing can take some time with a large group – the bridge does swing a fair bit and people concerned by heights may find this challenging. The bridge spans 100 metres, giving great views of the river below. On the far side, step off the bridge onto the large rock platform.

6 From the northern side, walk up the timber steps through the dense forest past the *Bowtells Bridge* sign. At the top of these steps, the track bends left then leads along the side of the hill for 500 metres, crossing a few gullies and climbing up and down a series of timber steps before passing between a couple of fence posts. Here you continue

down a fairly steep series of timber steps, enjoying the sounds of whipbirds, to a pleasant clearing and intersection marked with a *Private Land – No Camping* sign.

Turn right to follow the *Camping Ground – 500 metres* sign up the timber steps. The track soon bends left and follows the side of the hill for about 130 metres to pass through a gate with a *Welcome* sign. Continue along the clear track for another 70 metres to an intersection with the timber path just below the Six Foot Track Lodge. (This lodge offers a very pleasant alternative to camping at only $45 per person per night - for more details, turn this book over and go to page 32.)

7 Continue straight past the Six Foot Track Lodge access path, following

the clear track for 30 metres to cross a small gully, then climb over a fence using a stile. Turn right and follow the track for almost 50 metres to a T-intersection with a wide trail, beside a private property gate and marked with several *Six Foot Track* signs.

Veer left following the *Camping Ground – 200 metres* sign gently down along the wide trail. After about 230 metres the trail flattens out and passes below the main camping area (on your right) marked with a *Coxs River Reserve* sign. About 30 metres past here, you come to a clear intersection with the dirt Glen Chee Road, marked with a *Six Foot Track* sign.

(To continue along the Six Foot Track, turn right here and follow the notes in the next walk: **Coxs River Campsite to Black Range Campsite**.)

2 Megalong Valley to Coxs River Campsite

Historic image of camping on the Six Foot Track

Points of interest – Coxs River Campsite and the Coxs River

Coxs River Campsite, on the Six Foot Track, is found on the western bank of the Coxs River. You will find a sheltered picnic table, water (rain tank or creek – treat before drinking either), toilet and a flat, grassed camping area with excellent access to the river. This campsite is all about the river: spend some time on the bank enjoying the clear evening air, surrounded by the high ridge lines as the water continues to carve its way through the granite and sandy riverbed. The campsite is used by people walking the Six Foot Track, but is also visited at times by people who have driven in using their 4WDs. It is a pleasant place to camp and the nearby river makes a great place to cool down on warmer days.

The Coxs River starts near Lithgow, running south-east as the main tributary for the Warragamba Dam. The Six Foot Track crosses the river on the slippery rounded stones or, when in flood, the long, metal Bowtells suspension bridge. The river provides some potentially nice swimming spots, with pools and interesting granite rock formations – be very careful if deciding to swim as it can be very dangerous after rain. Governor Macquarie named the river to honour William Cox (1764-1837), an early Australian pioneer, road builder and explorer.

3 Coxs River Campsite to Black Range Campsite

Following in the historic footsteps of generations before, this walk guides you through the middle section of the Six Foot Track. You have the chance to explore a wide variety of bushland, from the moist tree fern gullies of Little River through farmland to the dry open forests high on the ridge lines. Walking along a well-managed 4WD dirt road and crossing a few creeks, you will climb from 290 metres to 1200 metres above sea level starting from the banks of the Coxs River. There are some beautiful views towards the Katoomba escarpment from Kiangatha Yards, and the valley at Alum Creek and Little River provides a pleasant, cool spot to rest or camp. Black Range campsite is on the edge of a state forest. The campsite is nestled in a native forest, but nearby is a pine plantation that is worth exploring – keep an eye out for the beautiful (but poisonous) bright red mushrooms.

At a glance

Grade: Hard

Time: 8 hrs 30 mins

Distance: 19 km one way

Ascent/descent: 1310 metres ascent/400 metres descent

Conditions: Following a 4WD dirt road for the whole walk, little shade on the road; best avoided on hot days. A lot of uphill walking, steep in places. Some creek crossings where you are likely to get wet feet; may become impassable after rain.

GPS of start: -33.7433, 150.1787

GPS of end: -33.7551, 150.0484

View from Kiangatha Yards

3 Coxs River Campsite to Black Range Campsite

Getting there

Car: Car access is possible in a 4WD to the Coxs River Campsite. Follow the driving directions then tracknotes for the Black Range to Coxs River walk, which is the reverse of this walk. At times this can be a challenging drive and some four wheel driving experience is recommended. You may find it easier to walk from Megalong Road and organise a pick-up from Black Range.

Drive to Black Range Campsite: From the Great Western Highway about 11 kilometres west of Mount Victoria, turn onto Jenolan Caves Road following the *Jenolan Caves* sign. Stay on Jenolan Caves Road for 23.6 kilometres (passing through Hampton) and continue straight at the intersection with Duckmaloi Rd, where there are traffic lights and road closed boom gates. Keep following the signs to Jenolan Caves for another 8.8 kilometres to the signposted intersection with Boggy Creek Road (a dirt road on your right). Turn left here and follow the dirt road (it initially veers a little left) as it leads into the pine forest for 1.2 kilometres (passing a few side roads) to come to a large intersection. Turn left and then almost immediately right, following the *Six Foot Track Black Range Camping Ground* sign. Follow the dirt road for about 100 metres until you come to the signposted and fenced Black Range Campsite, on your right.

Walk directions

1 From the intersection on the lower corner of the Coxs River Campsite, follow the *Six Foot Track* sign, uphill along dirt passing alongside the Coxs River Campsite. (For more information about Coxs River Campsite, refer to page 23 on the previous walk.) At the top of the campsite pass around the metal gate to find a dirt road turning area. Follow the '*Six Foot Track*' sign downhill along the dirt Glen Chee Road for about 150 metres to cross the usually shallow Gibraltar Creek then continue uphill for another 150 metres

to pass close to a high-tension powerline tower (up the hill to your left) Continue up along the dirt road for 200 metres to cross a usually small creek then head under the high-tension powerlines to cross Gibraltar Creek again. These creeks may become impassable after heavy or prolonged rain, although they can also often dry up. From here the dirt

3 Coxs River Campsite to Black Range Campsite

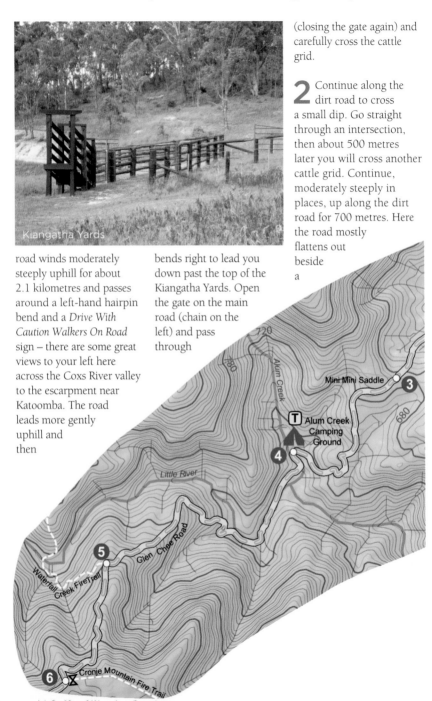

Kiangatha Yards

(closing the gate again) and carefully cross the cattle grid.

2 Continue along the dirt road to cross a small dip. Go straight through an intersection, then about 500 metres later you will cross another cattle grid. Continue, moderately steeply in places, up along the dirt road for 700 metres. Here the road mostly flattens out beside a

road winds moderately steeply uphill for about 2.1 kilometres and passes around a left-hand hairpin bend and a *Drive With Caution Walkers On Road* sign – there are some great views to your left here across the Coxs River valley to the escarpment near Katoomba. The road leads more gently uphill and then

bends right to lead you down past the top of the Kiangatha Yards. Open the gate on the main road (chain on the left) and pass through

grassy clearing, with views of the distant escarpment behind you. The road then leads more consistently and steeply uphill for 300 metres until suddenly flattening out at the top of Mini Mini Saddle, beside a clearing on your left.

3 Veer right and stay on the main dirt road

6FT arrow post, about 250 metres after leaving the clearing. Continue to walk downhill, moderately steeply in places, for 900 metres where the road bends left around the edge of a grassy clearing. About 40 metres further down the road, you pass an intersection with

downhill along the dirt road for just over 350 metres until coming to the signposted and gated Alum Creek Reserve campsite and toilet on your right.

4 Continue down along the dirt road as it bends left, and in just shy of 100

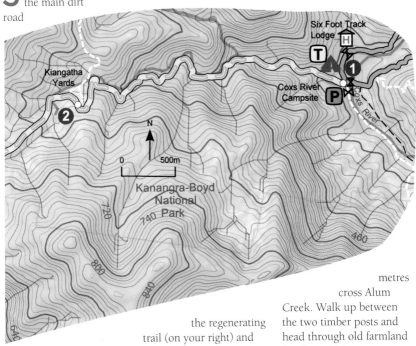

metres cross Alum Creek. Walk up between the two timber posts and head through old farmland for about 300 metres to pass a *Drive with Caution Walker on road* sign (facing away). Over the next 300 metres you continue through the old farmland,

as it leads along the side of the hill. The road leads past an open section of forest and starts to head downhill to pass a 20 km

the regenerating trail (on your right) and continue steeply downhill for just shy of 300 metres to turn left at the intersection at the other end of the regenerating trail. Continue more gently

3 Coxs River Campsite to Black Range Campsite

then walk beside pleasant Little River before crossing it at a point where it is usually shallow. You'll find yourself in a lovely mossy valley here, with plenty of tree ferns around the river. Just over 100 metres later this dirt road leads across the river again, and then again after another 110 metres. These creeks may become impassable after heavy

or prolonged rain, and also may become dry.

Continue straight, following the dirt road uphill for about 300 metres, then around a sharp right-hand bend and then left past the site of the old Kiangatha gates (now removed).

Continue walking fairly steeply uphill along the dirt road – another solid uphill slog has begun. After about 500 metres the road leads around a left-hand hairpin bend, then

150 metres later it briefly flattens out beside a large flat clearing on your left. Continue walking steeply uphill for 800 metres past a *Drive with Caution Walkers On Road* sign (facing away) to a Y-intersection with the signposted Waterfall Creek Fire Trail on your right.

5 Take the left fork at this intersection, following the arrow on the metal post up along the steep dirt road. After about 400 metres you pass a *20 km* 6FT arrow post then about 150 metres later the road flattens out briefly to pass a clearing on the top of the ridge (on your left). The dirt road continues to wind fairly steeply uphill for another 700 metres, with some distant views

Point of interest – Alum Creek camping ground

Signposted as Alum Creek Reserve, this flat grassy area, off the side of the dirt Glen Chee Road, is the 'extra' campsite on the Six Foot Track. The campsite is the least used and least developed of the three official campsites on the Six Foot Track, and makes a good place to stay if attempting the walk in two days, as it sits close to the middle of the whole walk. There is a pit toilet near the entrance and you will find the flat, green campsite is in a well-protected valley, surrounded by trees, with the small Alum Creek beside the campsite and the fairly reliable Little River down the road (treat water before use).

of the escarpment behind, before passing around a sharp left-hand hairpin bend. Just shy of 150 metres later the dirt road leads to a clearing at the top of Black Range, marked with a few *Six Foot Track* signs and the intersection with the signposted Cronje Mountain Fire Trail. Well done

– that is the main climb finished!

6 Veer right, following the 6´t arrow post generally west along the main dirt Black Range road. The road follows the top of the ridge line and undulates along the ridge for 2.1 kilometres, moderately steeply in a few short sections.

It passes through a pleasant, wooded forest and past a few large ant mounds until leading up to the signposted intersection with Moorara Boss Fire Trail on your left.

7 Keep walking straight ahead, following the 6´t arrow post gently uphill, staying on the dirt Black Range Road and still following the main

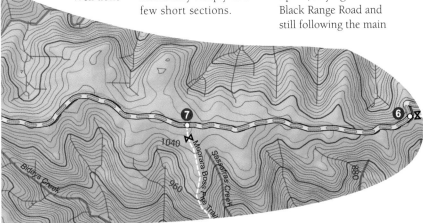

3 Coxs River Campsite to Black Range Campsite

Near Kiangatha Yards

ridge line. After about 100 metres you walk past a small dam on your left. Keep your eyes up looking for koalas – although we at Wildwalks are yet to see any, one walker told us they saw a koala along this section. You are more likely to spot some glossy yellow-tailed black cockatoos. Continue through the pleasant open forest for 2.3 kilometres before heading up a short steep section. About 900 metres from the top of this steep section the road leads fairly gently up to an intersection with the signposted Warlock Fire Trail on your left.

8 Continue straight on, following the arrow on the metal 6˙t post and staying on the dirt Black Range Road. After just shy of 100 metres this road splits in two for a short distance then almost 400 metres later comes to an intersection with the signposted Beefsteak Creek Fire Trail on your right.

Once again, continue straight ahead, following the 6˙t arrow uphill along the main dirt road. Soon the road leads up another short steep rise then more gently along the ridge for 400 metres to pass an intersection marked

with a metal *Kanangra Boyd National Park* sign. Continue along the main dirt road for another 1.2 kilometres to pass a short trail on your right (this leads into a clearing that has been used as a campsite). Here the dirt road continues gently uphill for 500 metres where you will find an intersection with a faint trail on the left, just before the clearing and pine forest.

9 Continue straight on, heading gently uphill along the main dirt road, towards the clearing. After about 80 metres the dirt road leads past a *Black Range Fire Trail* sign then about 25 metres later comes to the edge of the clearing and an intersection with another trail. Here you continue straight ahead, gently up along the dirt road, for 400 metres where the road bends right and comes to a T-intersection on the edge of the pine forest.

10 Turn left, following the 6˙t metal arrow post downhill along the dirt road, keeping the main pine forest to your right. (You're likely to spot eastern yellow-tailed black cockatoo along this section of the walk - for more information, turn this book over and go to page 17.) After about 250 metres you come to a clear four-way

Little River

3 Coxs River Campsite to Black Range Campsite

Little River

intersection marked with several *Six Foot Track* signs, and some powerlines on your left.

11 Turn left, following the *Six Foot Track - Black Range Camping Ground* sign gently downhill and under some powerlines along the wide trail. After about 50 metres you walk past a *Drive*

With Caution Walkers On Road sign, then another 50 metres later you come to an information sign in front of the signposted and fenced Black Range Camping Ground on your right. (To continue along the Six Foot Track, keep going straight ahead here and follow the next set of notes: **Black Range Campsite to Jenolan Caves.**)

Camping activities – How to spot possums

After sunset, with a fairly low-powered torch, stand a few metres from the base of a large gum tree, holding the torch close to your head. Point your torch up and look around the tree for the gleams of light that reflect from the back of the possums' eyes. Try to keep quiet and listen for movement in the trees to help you find your possums. In this way you can also spot most nocturnal animals and even frogs (although you may need to crouch down for them), and you may also come across the green eyes of spiders!

3 Coxs River Campsite to Black Range Campsite

Point of interest – Black Range camping ground

Black Range camping ground is a fenced campsite beside the Six Foot Track, and is also accessible by car. The well-maintained and signposted campsite has a couple of sheltered picnic tables, toilets, rainwater tank and an information board with map. The campsite is in a large fenced grassy area, with a stand of native trees. In the evening and early mornings you may find a few of the local wallabies grazing around the campgrounds. The tank water is quite reliable but the tank can become empty during long dry spells or through vandalism; please treat before use. A sign reminds campers that this is a Fuel Stove Only area – no camp fires.

4 Black Range Campsite to Jenolan Caves

This walk covers the southernmost section of the Six Foot Track. Starting from the Black Range Campsite in the state forest, you will follow a series of trails through native bushland before crossing Jenolan Caves Road. Keep an eye out while walking for kangaroos, wallabies – and, if you are lucky enough, some echidnas. After crossing the road you walk through some pleasant gullies before passing Jenolan Caves Cottages. Here you start heading down into the McKeown Valley, steeply towards the end, to finally pass the majestic Carlotta Arch and finish at the grand Caves House. The spectacular, ancient Jenolan Caves provided the motivation to build the Six Foot Track more than a century ago, and the limestone caves and the beautiful natural surroundings still draw in tourists from all around the world today – see the box at the end of this walk for information about cave tours.

At a glance

Grade: Medium

Time: 3 hrs 30 mins

Distance: 10.1 km one way

Ascent/descent: 330 metres ascent/720 metres descent

Conditions: Best avoided on very hot days. There are a few normally dry gullies that can get wet and muddy after rain. Steep, loose rocky section near the end of the walk.

GPS of start: -33.7551, 150.0484
GPS of end: -33.8203, 150.0212

Getting there

Bus: Trolley Tours has a $50 one-way deal from Jenolan to Katoomba designed for bushwalkers. The bus leaves the caves at 3 pm daily and takes about one and a half hours to get to Katoomba town centre (about a one-minute walk from the train station). Tickets must be pre-booked and paid for by phoning 1800 801 577, or through their website. Trolley Tours can also often organise a special drop-off at waypoint 3, where the Six Foot Track crosses Jenolan Caves Road.

Car to Black Range: From the Great Western Highway about 11 kilometres west of Mount Victoria, turn onto Jenolan Caves Road following the Jenolan Caves sign. Stay on Jenolan Caves Road for 23.6 kilometres (passing through Hampton) to continue straight ahead at the intersection with Duckmaloi Road, where there are traffic lights and road closed boom gates. Keep following the signs to Jenolan Caves for another 8.8 kilometres to the signposted intersection with Boggy Creek Road (a dirt road on your right). Turn left here and follow the dirt road (it initially veers a little left) as it leads into the pine forest for 1.2 kilometres (passing a few side roads) to come to a large intersection. Turn left and then almost immediately right, following the *Six Foot Track Black Range Camping Ground* sign. Follow the dirt road for about 100 metres until you come to the signposted and fenced Black Range Campsite, on your right.

Car to Jenolan Caves: Similar to above, but do not turn off Jenolan Caves Road, keep driving down the winding road, through the grand archway and you will pass Caves House (on your left). There is free parking further along the road. The last section of this road is one-way heading into the valley from 11:45 am to 1:15 pm every day (to make it possible for buses). If you want to drive out during this time you will need to go via Oberon.

Point of interest – Black Range camping ground

The well-maintained Black Range camping ground is a fenced campsite beside the Six Foot Track, and is also accessible by car. For more information, refer to the box in the previous walk on page 33.

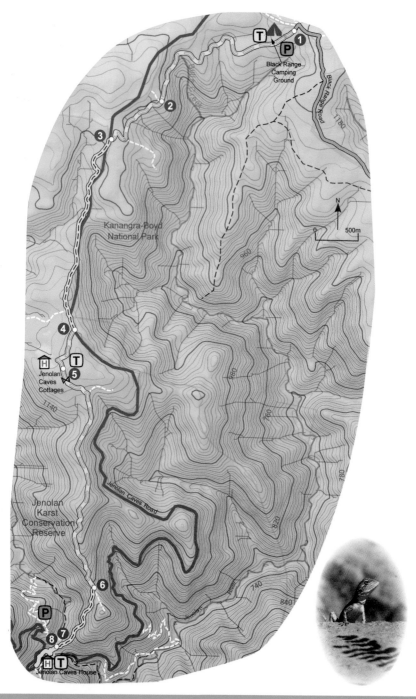

Australian reptiles – Snakes

You may be lucky enough to spot a snake or two on your walk. We had our closest encounter with a red-bellied black snake whilst writing this book, when one of us stepped on the poor thing – it was uninjured, don't worry! Some people use the fear of snakes as an excuse for avoiding stepping outside, but with some healthy respect we can get along well with these creatures. Snakes are scared of people and will generally run away when they feel the vibrations of your approaching footsteps. They are generally more active when it is warmer and you will see them sunning themselves on the track. If you do see one, just stop and wait a safe distance back – they will move soon enough.

Our close encounter happened on a warm day – but soon after a short and unexpected cold shower passed through, near Jenolan Caves. The poor snake was trying to warm up and it was too cold to run when it felt us coming. We weren't watching where we were stepping, but fortunately there was no harm done – this photo is of the actual snake. If he had bitten one of us, the first aid (see page 68) is very effective, so we could have waited until medical help arrived. One or two people die each year in Australia from snakebites, however generally they get bitten trying to kill the snake then ignoring the first aid advice.

Walk directions

1 From the information sign in front of Black Range Camping Ground, follow the *Six Foot Track* sign along the dirt road gently downhill, initially keeping the campsite to your right. Almost immediately pass around the green metal grate then past the *walkers next 3 km*

sign, after about 100 metres you leave the fenced edge of the campsite and come to an intersection with a management trail (to your left), and a 6FT arrow post pointing straight ahead.

Continue straight on, following the 6FT arrow post gently downhill along the wide management trail

through the tall native forest. After almost 200 metres, you pass a *10 km* 6FT arrow post. About 400 metres later the trail bends right and leads you more steeply downhill for about 200 metres, then bends left, this time crossing the upper reaches of Bulls Creek in a pleasant ferny gully.

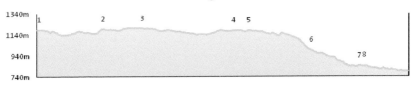

4 Black Range Campsite to Jenolan Caves

Continue along the trail, heading uphill past a few more 6FT arrow posts for about 500 metres to a clearing at the top of the ridge. Here the trail bends and leads downhill for 250 metres, through tall, open eucalypt forest with a scattering of pine trees, and a ferny understorey which is home to many birds. It then veers left at an intersection with a faint trail (on your right).

Continue along the main trail, moderately steeply uphill, keeping the valley on the left for just shy of 300 metres. Head up a noticeably steeper section, past a few out of place Telstra posts, for about 250 metres. Just as the trail start to flatten out again you come to a clear intersection with a trail on your right.

2 Continue straight ahead, following the 6FT arrow post downhill along the clear trail. After about 50 metres the trail bends right then leads you fairly steeply downhill for 250 metres to a pleasant gully. The trail then gently undulates along the side of the hill for 300 metres and arrives at a T-intersection, marked with a 6FT arrow post pointing right.

Veer right and follow the arrow gently uphill along the wide trail. After about 120 metres this trail bends left at a large grassy clearing. Just over 100 metres later you pass a *Road Ahead* sign and come to a larger clearing and gravel stockpile beside the sealed Jenolan Caves Road.

3 Continue straight ahead and cross Jenolan Caves Road – take care with traffic. Veer a little left to follow a 6FT arrow post down along the narrow track. From here walk past a *Road Ahead* sign (facing away) and meander along the side of the hill for about 300 metres before turning right, following a 6FT arrow post down some timber steps. After another 40 metres you cross a pleasant ferny gully and a small creek on a flat timber plank bridge.

The track continues along the side of the gully and up more timber steps for about 100 metres before flattening out and heading around the side of the hill for another 200 metres. It then brings you to the side of the road where you walk just behind the safety barrier for about 30 metres, then leave the road and head around the side of another small hill for 120 metres. Turn right and follow another arrow post down some timber steps for about 80 metres, and cross a gully with tall eucalypt trees on a flat timber plank bridge. Climb up more tim-

ber steps for about 40 metres where the track flattens out in view of the road. Turn right to head around the side of a small hill for 40 metres before once again turning right and following the 6FT arrow post down timber steps across a ferny gully. Then head up the hill for 130 metres to the large blue *Jenolan Caves Welcome* sign.

The track now widens into an old trail, and follows fairly close to the road and powerlines for 400 metres before bending right to lead up over a pleasantly wooded hill for about 600 metres, passing a *5 km* 6FT arrow. You then head downhill and walk along the side of a re-vegetating clearing and come back to the road once again. From here, follow the track, keeping the road a short distance to your left for 150 metres to an intersection with a driveway near a large blue *Jenolan Caves Cottages* sign.

4 Veer right and follow the *Cottages* sign along the driveway past the *20 km/h* speed limit sign, initially keeping the office/house to your left. The driveway leads over a small rise then heads downhill for about 300 metres to pass a toilet block. Follow the driveway as it bends left and continue beside the clearing to arrive beside the cottages.

Blue Lake

4 Black Range Campsite to Jenolan Caves

Located 9 kilometres from Jenolan Caves by road, Jenolan Caves Cottages offers eight well-presented self-contained timber cottages for guests to stay in. Each is fully insulated and furnished, with lounge, kitchen, two bedrooms and linen. There is a large flat grassy area in front with a children's playground, where you are more than likely to spot kangaroos grazing. For more information call Jenolan Caves on 1300 763 311. The cottages have a two-night minimum stay and prices are from around $180 per night per cabin. You will find a toilet just before the main car park.

5 Continue on, gently uphill along the driveway, for about 60 metres and then walk around the metal gate beside the *Six Foot Track* sign. Follow this mostly flat trail for 350 metres through tall, wooded native forest to a T-intersection marked with a *Kia-ora Hill Fire Trail* sign. Turn right and follow the *Six Foot Track* sign gently down along this trail for about 300 metres to a fairly large flat clearing. The trail continues generally downhill along the ridge line for 1.5 kilometres then moves to the side of the steep valley on your right. The trail begins to become steeper, then after 400 metres it leads you down a particularly steep, slippery rocky section for about 600 metres. Here the trail flattens out on a saddle and Y-intersection marked with a *Mt George* sign (pointing ahead).

6 Veer right to follow the *Six Foot Track* sign downhill along the narrowing track, enjoying the views into steep, wide McKeown Valley to your right. After about 25 metres the track leads between two timber posts and continues fairly steeply down the side of the valley for 500 metres, with glimpses to the cave buildings. The track flattens out a bit and heads under a solid gum tree, then leads you downhill for another 300 metres to cross a narrow limestone saddle where there are beautiful views down to Blue Lake on your left. Platypus can be spotted in this lake, though perhaps not from this height! (For more information about animals around Jenolan Caves, turn this book over and go to page 12.) You then descend some timber steps for about 50 metres

to a T-intersection with a gravel footpath.

7 Turn left and follow the *Caves House* sign gently downhill along the gravel path a short distance, arriving at an intersection and fenced lookout on your left near Carlotta Arch, a large and spectacular cave remnant overlooking Blue Lake.

8 Almost there! Follow the *Caves House* sign gently uphill along the stone path. The path leads over this small rise to a view into another valley. Follow this footpath as it now begins to zigzag fairly steeply downhill for 150 metres beside the limestone cliffs, passing views down to Caves House, past a bench seat to a *Caves House* information sign. The path continues more gently downhill for another 100 metres past the Grand Arch information sign (and view of the Arch) then just over 30 metres later to the *Southside Show Caves* information sign. You can almost taste the burgers now, so stay on the footpath for another 80 metres and down the steps to the side of Jenolan Caves Road, opposite Caves House, where a *Six Foot Track* sign points up the steps. This is the official end of the Six Foot Track – well done, you did it! The Trolley Tours bus leaves from the bus parking area down the hill. Follow the main road about 100 metres downhill, past a couple of buildings, to the parking station on your left, just before the entrance to the Grand Arch.

Point of interest – Jenolan Caves & Jenolan Caves House

No walk on the Six Foot Track is complete without seeing some of the spectacular underground scenery at Jenolan Caves – after all, the track was built to allow access to these majestic places. Give yourself some extra time to join a guided or self-guided cave tour. These spectacular limestone caves have been a popular tourist destination since the late 19th century. There are daily tours and activities – you will need to book into a tour to gain access to most of the caves. Call 1300 763 311 for more information. If you are short on time, make sure you walk through the Grand Arch and have a quick explore of the limestone formations. If you arrive here early enough you can squeeze in a tour before you go home, or better still stay the night and give yourself time to enjoy the larger cave tours.

Jenolan Caves House, built in 1898, is a heritage-listed building with a variety of accommodation options, and other services for visitors to the caves. Jenolan has two licensed restaurants: Trails Bistro is open from breakfast onwards and closes early evening, and serves a range of light meals including sandwiches, salads and hot food; Chisholm's Restaurant is open each morning for breakfast and each evening for dinner from 6 pm. Essential items and souvenirs may be purchased from Things Jenolan, located on the ground floor of Caves House. For more information, call Jenolan Caves on 1300 763 311. Accommodation ranges from $70-$500 per night for two people, from bunk house to premium rooms with ensuite.

About the Six Foot Track

A touch of history

The history of the Six Foot Track goes back millions of years, a long time before people and even dinosaurs walked this land. Without the geological events that led to the creation of Jenolan Caves, this track would never have been built. The geology also explains the grand topography of the mountains and the granite boulders scattered along the Coxs River. The following has been written to give you a feel for the land you are about to walk through – not just about how the track came to be, but also to give you a sense of the stewardship provided by the Gundungurra people and the other people who have come since.

Geological history

Geologists believe that the deep bedrock of the region was laid about 450 million years ago, and then flooded around 250 million years ago, as the sea inundated the area. The sea deposited sand, which hardened into the massive sandstone deposits that we associate with the Blue Mountains. As the area filled with sand, the water became shallower and the region became dotted with enormous swampy forests. These swamps led to the creation of the coal and shale deposits that are found in distinct layers throughout the Blue Mountains and the greater Sydney area.

There were apparently two significant volcanic eruptions in the Blue Mountains. The first of these occurred around 200 million years ago, as dinosaurs roamed the forests, and saw hundreds of volcanos and dykes carve out an entirely new landscape. The more recent volcanic event, 20 million years ago, saw an enormous lava flow (up to 60 metres deep) flow through the primitive landscape. This volcanic activity created some of the igneous rocks of the region: the granite that dominates the Coxs River valley, and the basalt extrusions which are also found through the mountains.

The region was then lifted by pressure deep below the surface, followed by a huge amount of erosion which removed much of the lava sheet from the Blue Mountains, leaving the basalt-capped mountains whilst allowing the deep sandstone gorges and canyons to be carved out by the creeks and rivers.

About the Six Foot Track

In 2006, Jenolan Caves was dated as 360 million years old by the CSIRO. This new discovery, suggesting the caves are much older than originally thought, may lead to a re-thinking of some of these dates, but what is a few million years between friends?

The Gundungurra people

There is plenty of evidence that the Megalong Valley and many of the areas around the Six Foot Track have been inhabited and cared for by the Gundungurra people for around 20 000 years. The Gundungurra people knew of Jenolan Caves and called it "Binoomea", meaning "hole" or "dark places". Archaeological evidence suggests that the Six Foot Track was built on routes used by the Gundungurra people, including sections along the Coxs River and the Black Range.

There are Aboriginal archaeological sites along the Six Foot Track that are not publicly promoted in an effort to protect them. Unfortunately some of these sites were disturbed in 2012 when Glen Chee and Black Range roads were upgraded.

The Gundungurra are well known for their practice of burying their dead in an upright position. Some particularly important people were also wrapped in bark and placed inside a tree hollow. Along with many others, the Gundungurra were badly affected by flu and other disease outbreaks. There was a particularly bad flu epidemic in 1846, killing many people.

Jenolan Caves

James McKeown, an alleged bushranger, is likely to have been the first European to visit Jenolan Caves, but the first documented visit was by James Whalan in 1838, when he and his brother were searching for Mr McKeown. James and his brother Charles explored some of the caves in the area, then in 1866 the caves were put under direct government control and Jeremiah Wilson was appointed caretaker of a few caves the following year. Unfortunately there was a lot of damage done to the cave formations and decorations in this time until 1872, when it became illegal to damage the caves, thanks to the legislation tabled by John Lucas.

In 1880 the caves started becoming a popular tourist destination, with the name "Jenolan" adopted in 1884. Caves House was built in 1898 and has been extended several times since. As the caves grew more popular, the slow and difficult access became an issue. Many people

About the Six Foot Track

came via a steam train from Sydney to Tarana Railway Station, and then travelled by horse and buggy along the rough coach road to the caves. The total journey could take 24 hours.

Today, the Caves are a thriving tourist destination, and the journey from Sydney takes only 3 hours by car. There are several guided tours daily, as well as kids' holiday activities and music performances inside the caves. Visit www.jenolancaves.org.au or phone 1300 763 311 for more information.

The Six Foot Track

"[The track is] steep in places, but the romantic beauty of the surroundings amply compensates for the roughness of the ground."
Blue Mountains Railway Tourist Guide, 1894

At the end of March 1884, a government-led expedition set off to find and mark a route, suitable for horses, linking Katoomba to Jenolan caves. They started by following a steep pass off Narrow Neck, but then decided that Nellies Glen provided better access to the valley. It took the small team a total of 11 days to mark out the entire route from Explorers Tree, down Nellies Glen, across the Coxs River, along the Black Range and down to Jenolan Caves – a very impressive effort!

The government then funded the construction of the track to the tune of £2,500. Once completed, the ride from Katoomba to the caves was less than eight hours.

In 1892 the Glen Shale Mine opened and the Megalong Village grew very quickly beside the Six Foot Track. The village disappeared even more quickly five years later, when the mine closed and the residents disassembled their houses to move them.

Soon after, a massive fire in the valley destroyed most of the remnants of the village.

A number of Aboriginal people lived on the edge of this village. They held a corroboree in the hall in 1896 and also played cricket as members of the Coxs River team, with the other teams in the region.

At the end of the 1880s and the early 1900s, a few families settled along the Coxs River near the Six Foot Track crossing. The Dyson family built a house and small farm on the east side of the crossing and the O'Reilly family on the western side. The Lynch family also built themselves a house in their land near the now Six Foot Track Lodge. The ruins of some of these are still visible but are on private property, off the main walk. A fire and a rabbit plague in the early 1900s meant that many people left this valley for Katoomba and other places.

In the early 1900s new roads were built in the area, providing faster access to the caves, and with the motorised car becoming more popular the Six Foot Track was getting much less use by the 1930s.

Early groups took packhorses

About the Six Foot Track

Over the years, sections of the track were developed into roads and fire trails. Other sections were claimed by farmers or reclaimed by the bushland. In the 1960s it seemed like a good idea to fill Nellies Glen and build a fire trail down through the canyon. However the idea soon proved unviable. Much of the vegetation and the Six Foot Track pathway was covered in the canyon. The forest is now reclaiming this canyon again.

The Modern Six Foot Track

The Six Foot Track, as we know, love and walk it today, was re-established in 1984—5 by the Orange Lands Office to celebrate the track's 100th birthday. The track now follows as closely as possible to the original route, and the department has installed stiles, signage and campsites to make the journey more enjoyable for walkers.

This is now a very popular walk, with many people enjoying this as their first overnight hike, whilst others enjoy sections as day walks. Today the walk is managed by the Six Foot Track Heritage Trust.

Further reading

For more about the Six Foot Track, the following websites make for interesting reading:

Geological History of the Blue Mountains
www.comleroyroad.com/geological—history.html

Gundungurra Tribal Council
www.gundungurra.org.au

Jenolan Caves Historical & Preservation Society
www.jenolanhistory.org.au

Another interesting read is *A Correct and Faithful Account of a Journey to Fish River Caves*, written in 1886 and edited by Dr Jim Smith in 2012. This book is an edited reprint of the 1886 account of the journey undertaken by seven people, including the first three women to walk the Six Foot Track. This diary was written by Alfred Allen and includes historically important, interesting and sometimes amusing accounts of their journey. This new printing of the diary includes many drawings and photographs. Dr Jim Smith, a Blue Mountains historian, has breathed extra life into this account by including a detailed commentary.

Track closures

All tracks are susceptible to closures for many reasons. Help land managers and save your frustration by checking track and closure information prior to setting out.

Significant closures or changes to the Six Foot Track may be noted at www.sixfoottrack.com. Due to major floods & fires (as well as the pandemic) between 2020-22 there have been significant road and track closures at the start and end of the Six Foot Track. This has also effected accommodation and transport options available, so please stay flexible and plan ahead.

Information about closures on any National Park estate can be found at www.npws.nsw.gov.au or by phoning 1300 361 967.

Unless you can find out otherwise, the safest option is to assume parks are closed on days of total fire ban. Current ratings and fire bans can be found at www.rfs.nsw.gov.au or by phoning 1800 679 737. The Six Foot Track passes through two fire regions. The Katoomba side, east of the Coxs River, is the Greater Sydney Region fire area, the western half (Jenolan end) is in the Central Ranges fire area.

Track changes

This book and its maps are based on how the walk was signposted at the end of 2018. Tracks and the surrounding environments do change. Changes occur for many reasons, so keep your eyes peeled and follow the local official signs. Notices about any significant changes

About the Six Foot Track

may be posted along the walk and on the websites mentioned above. Each walk in this book is also found on www.wildwalks.com; please leave your comments about changes there and read other walkers' comments. We enjoy hearing of other people's adventures and suggestions – you can email us at matt@wildwalks.com.

The website www.sixfoottrack.com has been created along with this book to support you on the track. It provides you with information in a different format that will also help you to plan your journey.

Using the tracknotes

Different people will use these notes in different ways. The Six Foot Track is generally well signposted, so you could just follow the signs and see what comes your way, but generally it's a good idea to be a little more prepared. As you read these notes, you will be able to picture what the walk will be like and how to prepare yourself. The notes will also act as a helpful guide on the day; you may want to flick through the notes at a rest break to remind yourself of what is coming up. If you are unsure which way to go, reviewing the notes from the last place where you knew where you were can be very helpful.

The maps in this book help with reading the notes and give a good sense of the journey. However, we recommend that you also carry topographical maps and keep a track of where you are. Even though the Six Foot Track is well signposted, tracknotes are not enough for you to be able to navigate. Although you will probably not use your topographical maps, they become invaluable if something does go wrong and you need to find the nearest road.

About the Six Foot Track

There are three 1:25 000 topographic maps that cover all the walks in this book: Katoomba (89301s), Hampton (89304S) and Jenolan (89303N), available at most outdoor stores. These maps cover a wider area than can be included in this book. You can also download custom topographic maps for this and other walks from www.wildwalks.com, or find maps and a useful app on www.sixfoottrack.com.

Terminology used in this book

When chatting with people, we can sometimes use the same word but have a different understanding of what it means. This can lead to us being very confident in our misunderstanding! To avoid this, here are some common phrases and terminology used in this book. This will hopefully give a better sense of what you are reading about.

Track: A worn or cut section that is reasonably clear to follow and wide enough for one person.

Path: A hardened route for use by pedestrian or bikes – such as a concrete footpath or cycleway.

Trail: A narrow road that is generally closed to public motor vehicles, usually dirt or gravel and wide enough for several people side by side.

Unsealed (dirt) road: A public dirt or gravel road – may be rough in places.

Sealed road: A bitumen or concrete public road.

Creek crossing: Unless otherwise mentioned, creek crossings are not bridged and may involve getting wet feet. These may flood and become impassable for a time.

Perennial creek: Flows all year round, may become dry during extended dry periods.

Intermittent creek: Only flows for part of the year, will be marked on maps.

Ephemeral creek: Only flows for a few days or so after rain, will sometimes be marked on maps.

Stile: An A-frame style ladder made of steel on wood that allows you to climb over a fence fairly easily. Used instead of gates.

About the Six Foot Track

Fees

There are no specific fees for undertaking the Six Foot Track. Campsites are free to use; the tracknotes will mention if there are any extra charges. There are obviously some costs associated with undertaking the walk — you will need to pay for your transport, food, accommodation etc. — but you can spend as much or as little as you want.

Walking itineraries

There are several ways you can approach the Six Foot Track: as a series of day walks, as a weekend hike or as an inn-to-inn walk. If you are so inclined, you may even want to challenge Ben Artup's effort in completing the annual 45-kilometre Six Foot Track marathon in 3 hours and 15 minutes (details of the marathon below)!

If you are walking in a group, remember to consider the differing skill levels of the group. Everyone walks at different speeds. The walking times have been calculated in a consistent way and assume that you are fairly fit and carrying a pack. Remember that the times give a sense of actual time spent walking, and do not include rest time — always allow extra time to rest. Whatever pace you choose to walk this track, make sure you allow time to enjoy the natural beauty and historic atmosphere. The following suggests some possible itineraries to use as a guide when planning your adventure.

Short walks

You can complete the Six Foot Track as a series of three or four separate day walks, just by following each of the four sections separately. You will need to do some car shuffles or have someone helpful to drop you off and pick you up. To make transport easier and to avoid the 4WD trip down to the Coxs River you may want to join Walks 2 and 3 into one bigger day walk.

The four-day walks are reasonably short, however it is possible to break them into even smaller sections. However, access at these points along the track is often via a particularly rough dirt road or a long side track. By reading through the notes and looking at the maps you can see where there are extra road access points.

Overnight hikes

The most common itinerary for the Six Foot Track is the three-day overnight hike. There are two main campsites on the Six Foot Track, one on the Coxs River and another on Black Range. There is also a more basic campsite at Alum Creek (near the halfway mark of the walk). You will also find a roadside camping area a short side trip from where the Six Foot Track crosses Megalong Road. Consider your accommodation options before and after the walk — you may want to stay at Jenolan Caves or in Katoomba, for example. There are good options at each end, giving you more time to explore.

Katoomba – Jenolan Caves camping itineraries

Numbers shown in brackets indicate a walk waypoint. For example, 4(wp3) means Walk 4, waypoint 3.

Most common – 2 nights (3 days) tent camping

Days Plan	Km	Hrs	Walks
Explorers Tree to Coxs River Optional luxury – Stay at 6FT Lodge	15.7	6.25	1 & 2
Coxs River to Black Range	19	8.5	3
Black Range to Jenolan Caves	10	3.5	4

Weekend trip – 1 night (2 days) tent camping

Days Plan	Km	Hrs	Walks
Explorers Tree to Alum Creek	21.8	8.75	1 & 2 —> 3(wp4)
Alum Creek to Jenolan Caves	23	9.5	3(wp4) —> end of 4

(N.B. Day 2 is a big day, and you will need an early start and to be fit to get to Jenolan Caves in time for the bus.)

No hurry, steady pace option – 4 nights (5 days) tent camping

Days Plan	Km	Hrs	Walks
Explorers Tree to Old Ford Reserve	8.7	3.5	1 & Alt Route to OFR
Old Ford Reserve to Coxs River Optional luxury – Stay at 6FT Lodge	8	3.5	Return to track-head & 2
Cox River to Alum Creek	6.1	2.5	3 —> 3(wp4)
Alum Creek to Black Range	13	6	3(wp4) —> end of 3
Black Range to Jenolan	10	3.5	4

(N.B. You have the option of booking a stay at Jenolan Cottages to split the last day into two.)

About the Six Foot Track

Jenolan Caves – Katoomba camping itineraries

Numbers shown in brackets indicate a walk waypoint. For example, 4(wp3) means Walk 4, waypoint 3.

Most common – 2 nights (3 days) tent camping

Days Plan	Km	Hrs	Walks
Jenolan Caves to Black Range	10	4.25	1
Black Range to Coxs River Optional luxury – Stay at 6FT Lodge	19	7.5	2
Coxs River to Explorers Tree	15.7	7.25	3 & 4

Weekend Trip – 1 night (2 days) tent camping

Days Plan	Km	Hrs	Walks
Jenolan Caves to Alum Creek	23	8.5	1 —>2 (wp11)
Alum Creek to Explorers Tree	21.8	9.5	2(wp11) —> 3 & 4

No hurry, slow pace – 4 nights (5 days) tent camping.

Days Plan	Km	Hrs	Walks
Jenolan to Black Range	10	4.25	1
Black Range to Alum Creek	13	5	2—> 2(wp11)
Alum Creek to Cox River Optional luxury – Stay at 6FT Lodge	6.1	2.25	2(wp11) —> end of 2
Coxs River to Old Ford Reserve	8	4	3 & alt route to OFR
Old Ford Reserve to Explorers Tree	8.7	4.25	Return to track-head & 4

(N.B. You have the option of staying at Jenolan Cottages to split the first day into two.)

Inn-to-inn walking

Walking inn-to-inn is very popular in parts of Europe; it is an overnight hike, with a few extra luxuries like a comfortable bed and a lighter pack. With a small amount of pre-planning you can walk the Six Foot Track in this style, staying in accommodation each night. This style of walking is not for everyone, but if you are reading this and thinking "that sounds nice", then give it a go. Below you will find more information on the inns and some suggested itineraries. Inns will come and go and prices will change; make sure you book and chat with your host ahead of time.

Inn-to-inn walking needs some planning and communication. In your day pack you will need to carry all the normal things for a remote area day walk and some extra food and a change of clothes for the evening. If you like even more luxury and less weight in your pack, chat with your host about dropping off a bag before the walk.

When talking with your host, please respect their time; we hope they can support walkers on the Six Foot Track for many years to come. When making a booking, discuss what meals you will need. For an extra fee your host may be able to help with dinner and breakfast, and maybe even organise a packed lunch for you. Where you need to be picked up, organise an approximate time, then call as you approach the trackhead. You will need a Telstra NextG or satellite phone to have any hope of making phone calls. Try hard to not keep your hosts waiting. As with all longer day walks you should be prepared for an unplanned night on the track in case things go wrong.

Accommodation options

Katoomba

There are lots of accommodation options in Katoomba – here are a few between the train station and Explorers Tree. Check online for many more accommodation providers in Katoomba.

Blue Mountains Backpacker

Clean, large and easygoing backpackers with a good kitchen and living area. Bed in dorm from $27-$32 per night, private rooms from $89 per night.

144 Bathurst Road, Katoomba
T: (02) 4782 9630
Web: www.bluemountainsbackpackerhostel.com.au

The Flying Fox Backpackers

Smaller backpacker lodge, accommodation includes breakfast and internet. Dorm bed from $29 per person per night.

190 Bathurst Rd, Katoomba
T: (02) 4782 4226
Web: www.theflyingfox.com.au

About the Six Foot Track

Sky Rider Motor Inn

Closest accommodation to the Explorers Tree. $110—$250 per room per night.

302 Bathurst Rd (cnr Valley Rd), Katoomba
T: (02) 4782 1600
Web: www.skyridermotorinn.com.au

Megalong Valley

Although not specifically mentioned in itineraries or the track notes, there are two places that provide accommodation near the Six Foot Track on the west side of Megalong Road. They are both a short walk from the Six Foot Track.

Euroka Homestead

Lovely farm-based cottage and homestead building. 2-night minimum stay.

3-bedroom cottage, sleeps up to 10 people: $650 per night.
5-bedroom homestead, sleeps 18 people: $850 per night.

T: 0412 639 014
Web: www.eurokahomestead.com.au

Dryridge Estate

A winery that provides a well-presented lodge with great views. $295—$360 per night per couple. $50 per extra guest (two Queen rooms).

T: (02) 4787 5625
Web: www.dryridge.com.au

Coxs River

As well as the campsite on the Coxs River, there is accommodation at the wonderful Six Foot Track Lodge. The lodge is right beside the track if you take the swing bridge option over the Coxs River.

Six Foot Track Lodge

The lodge has 2 cabins, each of which can sleep 12 people in bunks. The cabins each have warm blankets, pillows, log fire, pizza oven, tank water and their own outhouse toilet. The lodge is available on Friday and Saturday nights only, at $59 per person, per night. You may be able to stay mid week if you pre book an entire cabin from $590 (12 people) Dinner/breakfast or lunch packs can also be organised for about $20pp.

E: 6ftrack.ecolodge@gmail.com
Web: sixfoottrackecolodge.com

Black Range

There is no accommodation actually on Black Range or within a short walk of the campsite, but there are a couple of great spots nearby, with friendly hosts that are happy to pick you up and drop you back the next day. This must be organised and booked before you start the walk, and you need to plan your pick-up from Black Range campsite.

Telstra NextG provides weak coverage in the area around the Black Range campsite. A phone with a Telstra 'Blue Tick' works best in rural areas such as this. Reception is better closer to Black Range and Jenolan Roads.

Duckmaloi Farm

A series of cottages and a house in a pleasant farm setting. Cottages boast a spa, slow combustion fire, kitchen, bathroom and balcony with views. Cottage from $189 per night, per couple. Each cottage can sleep up to 5 people.

54 Karawina Drive, Duckmaloi
T: 0435 931 249
Web: www.duckmaloifarm.com.au

About the Six Foot Track

Melaleuca Mountain Retreat

A pleasant series of cabins in a farmland setting with distant views. Cabins from $235 per night per couple and vary in size between 2—6 people.

935 Duckmaloi Road, Oberon
T: (02) 6336 1158
Web: melaleucamountainretreat.com.au

Jenolan Road

Jenolan Cottages

The Six Foot Track passes directly past Jenolan Cottages, about 5 km walk (9 km via road) from Caves House. There are 8 self-contained, 2-bedroom cottages, overlooking a grassy clearing where kangaroos graze, and there is a great kids' playground and BBQs. $180 per night per cabin, 2-night minimum stay.

T: 1300 763 311
Web: www.jenolancaves.org.au

Jenolan Caves House

Jenolan Caves House has a good variety of accommodation options and licensed restaurants. Accommodation ranges from $64—$235 per night, from bunk house to premium rooms with ensuite.

T: 1300 763 311
Web: www.jenolancaves.org.au

Katoomba – Jenolan Caves Inn-to-Inn itineraries

Numbers shown in brackets indicate a walk waypoint. For example, 4(wp3) means Walk 4, waypoint 3.

Standard 2 nights (3 days) – requires your host to drive you for 1 night

Days Plan	Km	Hrs	Walks
Explorers Tree to 6FT Lodge	15.2	6	1->2(wp8)
6FT lodge to Black Range Lift to and from accommodation	19.5	9	2(wp8)-> end of 3
Black Range to Jenolan Caves	10	3.5	4

2 nights (3 days) door-to-door

Days Plan	Km	Hrs	Walks
Explorers Tree to 6FT Lodge	15.2	6	1->2(wp8)
6FT Lodge to Jenolan Cottages	25	12.5	2(wp8) -> 3 -> 4 ->4(wp7)
Jenolan Cottages to Jenolan Caves	4.7	1.5	4(wp7) to end of 4

This option has a particularly long day 2. If you are fit, this is doable. This option gives you time to explore Coxs River on Day 1 and more time at Jenolan on Day 3. It also means you are walking door-to-door to your accommodation.

1 night (2 days) door-to-door

Days Plan	Km	Hrs	Walks
Explorers Tree to 6FT Lodge	15.2	6	1->2(wp8)
6FT lodge to Jenolan Caves	29.6	14	2(wp8) -> 3 & 4

This option has an even longer day 2, with a lot of uphill walking. If you are fit, and your pack is light, then this is doable, but you will need an early start and plenty of daylight. Unless you jog you are unlikely to make the bus out of Jenolan Caves that day, so it's best to book a night at Caves House. If you are fit enough to consider this option your walking speed will likely be faster as well.

Jenolan Caves – Katoomba Inn-to-Inn itineraries

Numbers shown in brackets indicate a walk waypoint. For example, 4(wp3) means Walk 4, waypoint 3.

Standard 2 nights (3 days) – requires your host to drive you for one night

Days Plan	Km	Hrs	Walks
Jenolan Caves to Black Range Lift to and from accommodation	10	4.25	1
Black Range to 6FT Lodge	19.5	7.5	2 & 3 -> 3(wp3)
6FT Lodge to Explorers Tree	15.2	7.25	3(wp3) – end of 3 & 4

About the Six Foot Track

2 nights (3 days) door-to-door

Days Plan	Km	Hrs	Walks
Jenolan Caves to Jenolan Cottages	4.7	2	1 -> 1(wp5)
Jenolan Cottages to 6FT Lodge	25	10	1(wp5) -> 2 -> 3(wp3)
6FT Lodge to Explorers Tree	15.2	7.25	3(wp3) -> end of 3 & 4

This option has a particularly long day 2. If you are fit, this is doable — most of day 2 follows a 4WD road. This option gives you more time at Jenolan at the start and time to explore Coxs River on the morning of Day 3. It also means you are walking door-to-door to your accommodation.

1 night (2 days) door-to-door

Days Plan	Km	Hrs	Walks
Jenolan Caves to 6FT Lodge	29.6	12	1 & 2 -> 3(wp3)
6FT Lodge to Explorers Tree	15.2	7.25	3(wp3) -> end of 3 & 4

This option has a long first day, with a lot of downhill walking on a 4WD road. Suitable only if you are very fit, you are used to walking long days and your pack is light. You will need an early start and plenty of daylight.

Guided walking options

If you are unsure of your skills, struggling to find others to join you, or just enjoy walking in a guided group there are two companies that provide guided walks on the Six Foot Track. This is a great option for people who just want to carry the basics in their pack, and have some-one else worry about food, tents and transport details. The exact prices and what is included in these tours will vary over time, please check with their websites for the latest offers.

Life's an Adventure

Try the pack free walking experience. A 3 day guided pack free walk from Jenolan Caves to Blue Mountains to maximise the views. The tour is all about the creature comforts. This guided walk is for those who want everything done for you, so you can focus on the walk. You do not have to carry your clothes or overnight bags for the entire tour, these will be transported each day. With Life's An Adventure you will carry as little as your water bottle, camera and lunch each day. You will spend one night at the Six Foot Track Bushwalkers Eco Lodge and one night in a Grand Classic room with ensuite at the Jenolan Caves House. BBQ lunch at the charming Dryridge Estate in the Megalong Valley. Great meals featuring local produce.

Web: www.lifesanadventure.com.au

Peak Potential

A 2-day all-inclusive weekend Six Foot Track walk (the full track), where you'll only need to carry a day pack. The light pack can make the walking experience and sightseeing more comfortable and enjoyable. There will be an accompanying support vehicle to transport your overnight gear to the eco lodge nestled back in bushland from the beautiful Coxs River. Enjoy the company of fellow adventurers and immerse yourself in the great outdoors and nature as we take care of all the finer details and planning.

The cost is around $650.00
Web: www.peakpotential.net.au

The whole walk in a day

For people who are very fit and used to walking long distances in a day, it is possible to walk the whole track in one day. We would encourage anyone undertaking this option to be prepared for a night out, just in case things don't go to plan. A creek may be impassable or an injury may slow you down. Whilst writing this book we met Harry, who joined us for dinner at Jenolan Caves, after completing the whole walk in a day. The next morning he re-walked the track back to Katoomba. This is nicknamed the 12 Foot Track!

The Six Foot Track Marathon

Starting with just 7 people in 1984 this annual event now attracts around 1000 runners each year. As there are now so many runners, there is a staggered wave start allowing competitors to pace out along the track. The race starts at Explorers Tree and follows the main track, crossing the Coxs River at the campsite and finishing outside Caves House. If you like to run — start training!

Web: www.sixfoot.com

About the Six Foot Track

Safety and comfort

The following are some tips to help make your time on the Six Foot Track safer and more enjoyable. It is not possible to teach all that is needed here; if you are not an experienced walker, please consider finding someone who is, or join a walking club. Walking with a competent bushwalker will help build your own skills, comfort and safety levels.

Think before you TREK is a bushwalking safety initiative between NSW Police and NPWS. The program promotes safe walking by helping people be better prepared and equipped.

T - Take adequate supplies of food, water, navigation and first aid equipment.

R - Register your planned route and tell friends and family when you expect to return.

E - Emergency beacons (PLBs) are available free of charge from NSW Police Force and NPWS.

K - Keep to your planned route and follow the map and walking trails.

- **Pull out if things aren't right**. It doesn't take much for a minor incident to turn major, especially if you are ill or the weather is not favourable. If things look wrong, please postpone your walk for another day.

- **Consider exit options**, in the event you need to pull out.

- **Choose your itinerary carefully**. Choose an itinerary that is suitable for you and your walking buddies. Walkers with heart, circulatory or breathing difficulties should be particularly cautious.

- **Eat well**. Walking is a key time to eat well, so take some time to plan your food and snacks. Making time to eat good food with friends is much better than ending up with fatigue from hunger. Fresh fruit will last if packed well and makes a perfect snack.

- **Wear sensible shoes**. Choose comfortable and sturdy shoes; avoid wearing brand new shoes. Look after your feet; if you feel a hotspot, take the time to prevent the blister before it grows. If your feet get wet crossing a river, try to dry them well before continuing.

- **Keep an eye on the weather**. The weather can change quickly. Be prepared for extreme conditions and always visit www.bom.gov.au ahead of time for forecasts.

About the Six Foot Track

- **Take great care on hot, dry days, and avoid walking at the peak of summer**. Consider the risk of bushfire and dehydration before heading into the more remote sections of this walk. Use alternate routes where signposted if you choose to walk on high fire danger days. Have a bushfire survival plan, and carefully consider cancelling your trip when fire danger is Very High or higher. Visit www.rfs.nsw.gov.au for more information. The walks east (Katoomba side) of the Coxs River are in the Greater Sydney Region fire area, and the western walks (Jenolan end) are in the Central Ranges fire area.

- **If you are planning on walking the Six Foot Track in winter, be prepared for snow and freezing temperatures**. Snow and temperatures below freezing are not rare events in winter.

- **Slip Slop Slap Seek Slide**. Slip on a shirt, slop on sunscreen, slap on a hat, seek shade, and slide on the sunnies. Visit www.cancer.org.au to learn more about protecting yourself from the sun.

- **Carry and know how to use a first-aid kit**. A remote area first-aid kit from an outdoor store is a great idea. Training in first aid, especially remote area first aid, is even more valuable and potentially lifesaving. Make sure you and your friends are carrying personal medication. If anyone in your group has asthma, severe allergies or other life-threatening conditions, make sure a few people understand the signs and the appropriate management plan. Know how and when to apply a pressure immobilisation bandage and how to help a person who is unconscious.

- **Carry a good insect repellent**. Always handy to relieve you of some critters such as ticks, leeches, flies and mozzies.

- **Walk in a group**. Some people enjoy walking alone, but it is much safer to walk with other people. If you choose to walk alone, then take extra precautions to deal with the significantly increased risk. Groups between four and eight people are ideal. Organised groups such as schools, scouts or guides need to book with the Six Foot Track Heritage Trust before starting the walk.

- **Stay together**. It is important to keep your group together; if something goes wrong, you have a much better chance of surviving in a group. Have each person in your group carry a whistle and use it to find each other if you get separated.

- **Tell someone where you are going**. Even on short walks, always make sure someone responsible knows where you are going, when to expect you back, and what to do if you are late returning.

About the Six Foot Track

- **Carry a mobile phone**. In an emergency dial 000 and be ready to explain where you are and what help you need. Telstra NextG network offers fair coverage on about half the walk. Pre-paid sim cards are available cheaply. Even a second-hand digital phone with no sim card can make an emergency call; if you don't own a phone, ask a friend to borrow theirs. Charge and conserve your battery.

- **Carry a PLB**. Please carry a Personal Locator Beacon (PLB, sometimes referred to as an EPIRB), or another satellite-based emergency beacon such as SPOT or an inreach2-way satellite communicator – they do save lives. These devices call for help in a life-threatening situation, and they work even when your mobile phone does not. A PLB offers a fast and reliable way to attract help; other devices like SPOT may be a bit slower, but offer additional handy functions. They may sound expensive, but only until you need one. Trigger your PLB if there is a threat of grave and imminent danger, and there are no other reasonable means of communication; always try your phone first. At Wildwalks we always carry a beacon with us in the bush, even on very short walks. Help will come, but it will take time; be prepared to wait for several hours, or maybe a few days depending on the weather.
FREE PLB hire is available from Katoomba Police station. Visit: www.police.nsw.gov.au/safety_and_prevention/crime_prevention/outdoor_recreation.

- **Be prepared for an unplanned night out**. On all walks, carry enough equipment, food and water to spend an unplanned night out. It doesn't have to be your best night's sleep, but you do need to survive.

Drinking water

Water is critical for life, and dehydration kills very quickly. Carry plenty of water, as many of the creeks do dry up. There are tanks or creeks where you can get water at each campsite on the Six Foot Track. Plan where you are going to get water from, and what you will do if you run low. Sterilise water from creeks and tanks by boiling or other system. It is possible (although very rare) for the tank at Black Range to dry up during long dry spells or through vandalism. The creek at Alum Creek campsite does dry up fairly often, but you can try Little River nearby which tends to hold water for longer. The Coxs River is a reliable water supply.

Water crossing

Take great care when deciding to cross a creek. During and after rain, creek levels may rise to a point where it is unsafe to pass. Even shallow, fast-moving water can be deadly.

If a creek is unsafe to pass, consider backtracking or camping out until it drops to a safer level. Many of the creeks now have bridges across them, although some crossings do become too dangerous to cross after heavy or prolonged rain.

About the Six Foot Track

Weather

Weather forecasts become less reliable the further they look forward, but are generally reliable for the first 24 hours. Check the forecast, and keep an eye on the weather as you walk. Avoid walking when there is a risk of thunderstorms. Great care is needed when walking in summer, due to the hot dry conditions, and generally it is more pleasant to walk in the spring and autumn. Check the UV index, weather forecasts and other handy information at www.bom.gov.au.

Average Temperature Range for Oberon

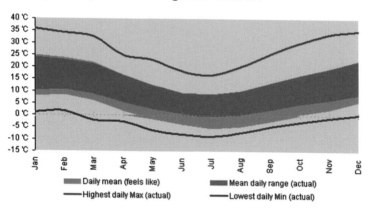

Average Rainfall Range for Oberon

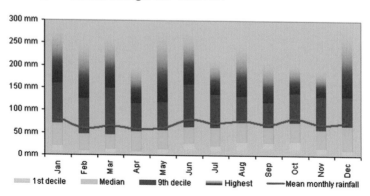

Average number of rainy days Oberon

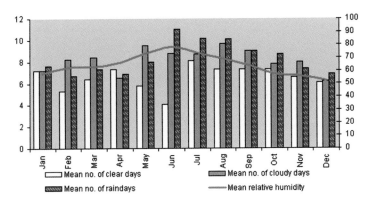

Data provided by BOM

A chill in the air

The air temperature is just one factor when considering how warm or cold it is. As a general rule on cooler days, the higher the wind speed, the colder it will feel and the faster your body will cool down. This windchill can be very dangerous on cold days. The following table gives you a sense of how quickly windchill affects the apparent temperature and the second table shows what that can mean to your body. An outer shell, such as a well-fitting, quality raincoat and over-pants provides some good protection from the wind.

Windchill Table

Air temperature (°C)

	Calm	4	2	-1	-4	-7	-9	-12	-15	-18
W	8	2	-1	-4	-7	-11	-14	-17	-21	-24
I	16	1	-3	-6	-9	-13	-16	-20	-23	-27
N	24	0	-4	-7	-11	-14	-18	-22	-25	-28
D	32	-1	-4	-8	-12	-15	-19	-23	-26	-30
	40	-1	-5	-9	-13	-16	-20	-24	-27	-31
km	48	-2	-6	-9	-13	-17	-21	-24	-28	-32
/ hr	56	-2	-6	-10	-14	-18	-22	-26	-29	-33
	64	-3	-7	-11	-14	-18	-22	-26	-30	-34

About the Six Foot Track

Windchill Temperature	Cold Threat
-6°C to 4°C	COLD. Unpleasant.
-17°C to -7°C	VERY COLD. Very unpleasant.
-28°C to -18°C	BITTER COLD. Frostbite possible. Exposed skin can freeze within 5 minutes.
-56°C to -29°C	EXTREMELY COLD. Frostbite likely. Exposed skin can freeze within 1 minute. Outdoor activity becomes dangerous.

Heat Index

On warmer days, higher humidity can increase the heat index to dangerously high levels. For example, if the temperature is 30 degrees but humidity is 40%, the temperature will feel as if it is 36 degrees.

The table below indicates the effect that high temperatures can have on people. (These values are for shady locations only; exposure to full sunshine can increase heat index values by up to 10°C.) Also, strong winds, particularly with very hot, dry air, can be extremely hazardous as the wind adds heat to the body. Regular rests and water on hotter days are critical.

Category	Classification	Heat Index/ Apparent Temp (°C)	General Affect on People in High Risk Groups
I	Extremely Hot	54°C or Higher	Heat/Sunstroke highly likely with continued exposure.
II	Very Hot	40°C - 54°C	Sunstroke, heat cramps, or heat exhaustion likely, and heatstroke possible with prolonged exposure and/or physical activity.
III	Hot	32°C - 40°C	Sunstroke, heat cramps, or heat exhaustion possible with prolonged exposure and/or physical activity.
IV	Very Warm	26°C - 32°C	Fatigue possible with prolonged exposure and/or physical activity.

Hypo and Hyperthermia

For our bodies to work well, our internal organs need to stay at a fairly constant 37°C. If your body gets too hot (hyperthermia), it starts to cook – this can rapidly cause severe damage and death.

If your body gets too cold (hypothermia), it becomes less co-ordinated and also risks death. As always, it is best to avoid these conditions by dressing appropriately and avoiding exposure to extreme temperatures. Eat well and drink plenty of water.

Too Hot:

Stop walking, rest and cool the person down as quickly as possible, but do not over-cool. Lay them in the shade, with minimal clothes – wet their clothes and fan them. Using water from a creek is fine, but do not over-cool them. If they are conscious, encourage them to drink water or sports drinks (never give alcohol).

Call for urgent emergency help if the person's body temperature is over 40°C, their skin is flushed and dry, they are behaving abnormally (or are unconscious) and/or any other sign that suggests they are in need of emergency medical aid.

Too Cold:

In the early stages, the person will feel cold and be shivering, they may be clumsy, slur their speech or act irrationally. Get shelter and protect the person from the wind, water and ground. Put dry clothing on them and lay them down on a sleeping mat in a sleeping bag (or wrap in a space blanket). Give the person warm, sweet drinks (never give alcohol).

Call for urgent emergency help if the person continues to get colder, stops shivering, becomes less conscious or any other sign that suggests they are in need of emergency medical aid. If the person does deteriorate to the point where they stop shivering then do not move them, instead gently warm them with your body heat and by having other people in the tent. Never use radiant heat (such as a fire) to heat someone who has stopped shivering, it is likely to kill them.

About the Six Foot Track

Things that bite

Ticks, leeches, dogs and snakes are fairly common in places on the Six Foot Track, but rarely cause any real grief.

Leeches rarely cause any issues to people. It's best to let the leech finish its dinner and drop off by itself. If you choose to remove the leech, there is little research, but there does seem to be greater risk of infection if you use salt, heat or other similar methods for removal. It seems safer to remove the leech by sliding your fingernail along your skin to break the leech's sucker seal, then flick it away and manage the small bleed. Austin Health suggests never pulling the leech off.

Although most tick bites cause minor or no symptoms, some can pose a serious threat to your health. At the end of your day, check for ticks especially behind your ears, the back of your head, groin, armpits and back of knees. NSW Health recommends the following: "Remove a tick as soon as possible after locating it. Use fine pointed tweezers and grasp the tick as close to the skin as possible. Gently pull the tick straight out with steady pressure. If you have difficulty, seek medical attention. Do not try to kill the tick with methylated spirits or any other chemicals. This will cause the tick to inject more toxins. If you have a severe infestation by larval stage ticks (often referred to as grass ticks) take a bath for 30 minutes with 1 cup of bicarbonate of soda." Some hospitals are now using olive oil to drown the tick before attempting to remove it.

As the Six Foot Track travels through farms and state forests, you may meet a few dogs along the way. Do not tease or approach any dogs, just let them be. The American CDC recommends that if you are approached by a dog acting aggressively, do not run, move, scream or maintain eye contact. If you are bitten, get to a safer location, manage the bleeding, clean the wound and seek medical attention.

You may also see snakes along the way, particularly in warmer months. Snakebites are rare; leave the snake alone and it will leave you alone. In the unlikely event of a snakebite, ensure everyone's safety first and maintain the casualty's airway/breathing if impaired. Apply a firm broad pressure immobilisation bandage to the bitten limb including fingers/toes. Splint the limb and ensure the casualty does not move. Seek emergency medical assistance to bring transport to the casualty. Do not give alcohol, food, or stimulants, and do not cut the wound, use a tourniquet, or clean the bite site. Be patient and reassure the casualty; the chances are they will be fine if you follow the appropriate first aid and seek medical help.

Biosecurity alert – Myrtle rust

Myrtle rust (*Uredo rangelii*) is a fungus, first detected in Australia on the central coast of NSW in April 2010. Myrtle rust can cause a very serious disease in Australian native plants in the Myrtaceae family. This includes plants like bottlebrushes, tea-trees and eucalypts. The fungus causes the plants' leaves to deform and it may kill the plant. Because this is newly discovered, the full extent of the disease is yet to be understood. The disease thankfully has not yet been found on the Six Foot Track, but it has been found in the Blue Mountains area.

Myrtle rust produces distinct powdery bright yellow (sometime orangey-yellow) spores on the leaves, stems, flowers and fruits. Lesions on the plant can be purple or dark brown. If you see an infected plant, do not touch it and never collect a sample. Take a photo and note your location. Call the Six Foot Track manager and tell them what you found. If there is any chance that you have come in contact with the fungus, change into fresh clothes and wash your hands, face and footwear to prevent it spreading. Clean your shoes with a 70% methylated spirits or benzyl alkonium chloride disinfectant.

There are other biosecurity risks to our unique bushland. After all bushwalks, it is always best to clean your clothes, shoes and equipment (included tent pegs) to prevent the spread of a wide range of these diseases.

You can learn more about myrtle rust by visiting www.dpi.nsw.gov.au/biosecurity/plant/myrtle-rust

"Dr Louise Morin ©CSIRO"

Navigation and staying found

The Six Foot Track is generally well signposted, but you still need to pay attention to your navigation. You always need to know where you are, in case you miss an intersection or need to call for help. Good navigation helps you have a safer and more enjoyable journey. The notes and maps will help, but you will still need to be aware of changes and be able to deal with emergencies.

A GPS unit is a helpful tool for finding your location. However, like compasses, they have their limits. The Wildwalks App gives you access to the high quality maps using the GPS in your phone.

Don't leave the main track, even if you are concerned that you're no longer on the correct track. "Bush-bashing" to try to find your way is hard work, very slow and dangerous. If you feel you have gone

About the Six Foot Track

the wrong way; stop, look at the maps and read the notes. It is often helpful to backtrack to the last place where you knew where you were. If you see someone, swallow your pride and ask for help; you might make a new friend.

In the unlikely event you find yourself really lost, then stop and stay put. Call for help and make yourself comfortable, visible and heard. If your phone does not work, remember that you have told someone responsible where you were going, and when you are due back. Trust that they will raise the alarm. If you wander about, it is likely to make a search harder. Even if your phone is out of range, try sending an SMS when holding the phone above your head. Sometimes a message will get through even when calls cannot. If sending an SMS, please, send it to someone who will act (000 does not accept SMS messages). Messages must be clear, with information about what help you need and where you are. If you have tried all reasonable means of getting help, and you feel your welfare is at risk, then you can use your PLB. Whatever means you use to raise help, it will probably take hours or maybe days; so conserve your energy, keep warm, dry and get comfortable. Avoid waiting next to moving water; it makes it harder to hear rescuers calling. Wait in an area providing the clearest view.

Leave no trace

Scars left by previous walkers not only detract from your experience but can leave long-lasting and sometimes irreparable damage to the environment. It is easy to point fingers, but at the end of the day, many of the scars are created by well-meaning people. Here are some tips to help you 'leave no trace' of your time on the Six Foot Track and surrounding walks.

Plan ahead and prepare:

Think about your group's goals and needs. Read though the tracknotes and study the maps. Phone the track co-ordinator if you have any questions. Consider weather conditions and creek crossings. Leave plenty of daylight to set camp. Clean your boots, clothes, tents, pegs etc. between trips to avoid spreading weeds and diseases. Try to keep group size between four and eight people.

About the Six Foot Track

Travel and camp on durable surfaces:

Stay on track – don't cut corners. Use existing campsites. In larger groups, rest on harder surfaces and established clearings, or spread along the track.

Dispose of waste properly:

Pack it in – Pack it out. Minimise packaging. Plan meals to avoid waste; especially avoid wet waste. Pick up all food scraps; even small amounts of food can impact on wildlife. Spend time searching for rubbish before leaving camp and rest stops. Carry out all rubbish, even if it is not yours, and have a dedicated rubbish bag for this purpose.

Consider hygiene. Gastroenteritis is very serious illness, especially in remote areas, and should be avoided. Carry and use alcohol-based handwash; it kills most bugs and you do not need water to rinse. Wash dishes and cooking equipment well, but ensure no soap or detergent is used within 100 metres of a waterway.

Use toilets where possible, and carry a small trowel for when needed. Where there are no toilets, bury waste in a 15 cm deep hole, at least 100 metres away from any water source and campsite. Use a small amount of plain toilet paper. There is a growing and recommended trend to carry toilet waste out using special tough bags or containers. Tampons and sanitary pads do not biodegrade well, and should be double-bagged and carried out. Urinate on a hard surface such as a rock then dilute with water. Always toilet out of view of the track and other people.

Leave what you find:

Let other people enjoy what you discover. Don't touch or walk on rock engravings, don't pick flowers or plants and respect the cost of infrastructure such as fences, signs and seats. Treat heritage items as though you are in an outdoor museum. Don't build cairns or mark the track in any way, and don't start new campsites.

Minimise campfire impacts:

Campfires can be enjoyable, but they are not always appropriate. The Black Range Campsite is a fuel-stove-only area; even though there may be existing fire scars, no campfires are to be lit here. Never light a fire or use a fuel stove on a total fire ban day; the Six Foot Track east of the Coxs River is in the Greater Sydney Region fire area, and the Jenolan side of the Coxs River is in the Central Ranges fire area. In the warmer

About the Six Foot Track

months, be prepared with meals that do not need cooking. There were over 150 bushfires caused by campfires in NSW last year – don't become a statistic. If you plan to light a fire, use an existing fireplace and keep the fire small. A small fire is better for cooking, less likely to get out of control and uses less timber. Minimise the amount of timber you collect and don't use dead hollow logs as they form important habitat for many small animals.

Respect wildlife:

Encounters with wild animals are special; enjoy them from a distance. If you see an animal, stop and wait to let the animal pass in its own time. Never feed, catch or pat wild animals. Let snakes be; trying to kill or catch them just increases your chance of being bitten. Please leave pets at home as the Six Foot Track passes through National Park land where pets are not allowed.

Be considerate of your hosts and other visitors:

The Six Foot Track travels across many different land tenures, both on public and private land. Be friendly to your hosts and land managers – say g'day and thank them if you see them. This walk is only possible because of so many people getting along; help promote a positive vibe on track with all the people you encounter. Smile!

About the authors and Wildwalks

The walks in this book have been diligently documented by the people at Wildwalks.

Matt McClelland

Having developed a love for bushwalking during scouts - the Six Foot track was one of Matt's first overnight walks. To share this passion for the outdoors Matt developed a Wildwalks.com and also hosts the community at bushwalk.com. For this book Matt wrote the tracknotes and text and produced the maps. For the companion website Matt also had fun developing the panoramic cameras system to image the whole walk.

About the Six Foot Track

Caro Ryan

Caro fell in love with bushwalking during a 3 day trip to the Budawang National Park in 1994. She is now a regular trip leader for the Sydney Bush Walkers club and the Bushwalkers Wilderness Rescue Squad (http://www.bwrs.org.au), where she is currently training as a Search Manager. Some of her favourite walking areas are the Wild Dogs Mountains in the Blue Mountains National Park and Kanangra-Boyd Wilderness Area. For this project Caro helped produce the companion website and was central in the production of the series of videos to help support people undertaking this classic walk. You can also follow Caro's blog and YouTube Channel at http://lotsafreshair.com - tips and tricks from an unexpected outdoors chick!

Geoff Malinson

Geoff was the first guy to climb all 26 peaks over 2000m in Australia in one go on foot. Loving long distance walks especially above tree line and back country skiing he has learned the art of packing very light. One of Geoff's greatest joys is sharing the outdoors with his wife and four kids. For this project Geoff was central to the production of the companion website and was the man behind (and in front of) many of the camera shots. You can follow Geoff's blog at http://geoffmallinson.com/

About Wildwalks

Wildwalks is a small team of professional bushwalkers, dedicated to making bushwalking more accessible and safer for our community. At www.wildwalks.com you will find useful information on hundreds of walks around NSW, including track notes, photos, walk grades, walking times, terrain profiles and more. The track notes are frequently updated and are integrated with information on weather forecasts, fire ratings and park closures. There are also printable versions of track notes that include topographic maps. You may be surprised to discover how many more walks there are near you. Please visit www.wildwalks.com to leave feedback on your walk, and read about other people's experiences.

About the Six Foot Track

About www.sixfoottrack.com

In creating this book we realised there was a need for a dedicated website to support people walking this iconic and popular walk; so we created www.sixfoottrack.com. The website is a great spot to connect with other walkers and keep up-to-date with new information about the Six Foot Track. Explore maps, more photos (including a lot of panoramic images), videos and extra tips on how to prepare for the walk. It is a great supplement to this book.

About www.bushwalk.com

If you are keen to connect with other bushwalkers in Australia or just have general questions about walking in this great country then drop in and visit www.bushwalk.com. The forum is a great community of around 5000 bushwalkers who are keen to chat about walks, gear and anything else bushwalking. Join in – would be great to chat with you there!

Photography Credits and Acnowledgements

Most of the photographs in this book were taken by the Matt McClelland from the Wildwalks team. Other images have been gratefully received from many keen walkers of the Six Foot Track.

Thank you to the Lang-Predavec family for the small image on the front cover (K-J), to Jesse Lomas for the main cover image, and to Bert Temme for the small image on the back cover (J-K).

Thanks also to John Merriman and Blue Mountains City Library for the historical images on pages 1, 23 and 45 (Katoomba to Jenolan) and page 41 (Jenolan to Katoomba). Thanks to Martin Stannard for the images on pages 3 and 22 (Katoomba to Jenolan); Kirsty Stewart for the images on page 25 (Katoomba to Jenolan) and page 27 (Jenolan to Katoomba); Veechi Stuart for images on pages 4, 8 and 20 (Katoomba to Jenolan); Thomas Ritter for images on page 33 (Katoomba to Jenolan) and page 25 (Jenolan to Katoomba); Jenolan Caves Trust on page 13 (Katoomba to Jenolan), and John Merriman for images on pages 15 and 48.

All photos remain copyright of the original photographer.

Index

Index

Woodslane Press

The Six Foot Track is just one of a growing series of outdoor guides from Sydney publishers Woodslane Press. To browse through other titles available from Woodslane Press, visit www.woodslanepress.com.au. If your local bookshop does not have stock of a Woodslane Press book, they can easily order it for you. In case of difficulty please contact our customer service team on 02 8445 2300 or info@woodslane.com.au.

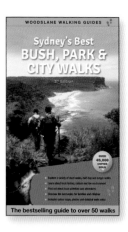

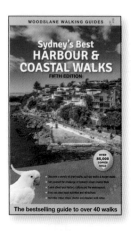

Titles include:

Blue Mountains Best Bushwalks

$32.99
ISBN: 9781925868678

Sydney's Best Bush Park & City Walks

$32.99
ISBN: 9781925403572

Sydney's Best Harbour & Coastal Walks

$32.99
ISBN: 9781925868623

The Great North Walk

$32.99
ISBN: 9781921874215

Best Walks of
The Illawarra

$32.99
ISBN: 9781925868456

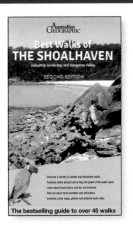

Best Walks of
the Shoalhaven

$32.99
ISBN: 9781925403558

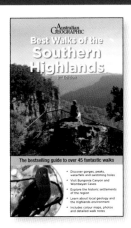

Best Walks of the
Southern Highlands

$32.99
ISBN: 9781925868111

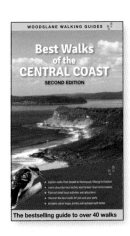

Best Walks
of the
Central Coast

$32.99
ISBN: 9781925403589

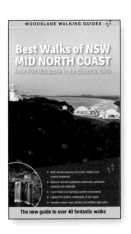

Best Walks of NSW
Mid North Coast

$32.99
ISBN: 9781922800008

Sydney for Dogs

$29.99
ISBN: 9781925403541

Notes

The Six Foot Track
Jenolan Caves to Katoomba

Updated **2nd** Edition

By
Matt McClelland and the
Wildwalks Team

in association with:

Dedication

To the next generation, particularly Eric and Laura. I hope that we take great care of these natural places, and I trust that you can pass them onto your children, in even better health. Let's not settle for sustainability but work towards a flourishing environment.

Woodslane Press Pty Ltd
10 Apollo St, Warriewood, NSW 2102
Email: info@woodslane.com.au
Website: www.woodslanepress.com.au

First published in Australia in 2013 by Woodslane Press
This second edition published in Australia in 2018 by Woodslane Press
Reprinted 2020, updated and reprinted 2023

A catalogue record for this book is available from the National Library of Australia

MIX
Paper from responsible sources
FSC® C001507

Printed in Malaysia by Times Offset Printing International.
Designed by Kasun Senaratne and Jenny Cowan.

Contents

Note: Turn this book over for tracknotes running from Katoomba to Jenolan Caves, and to read about the history of the track and to review itineraries.

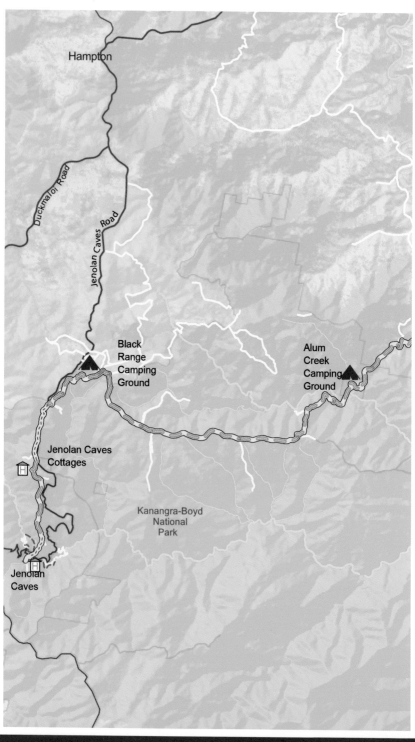

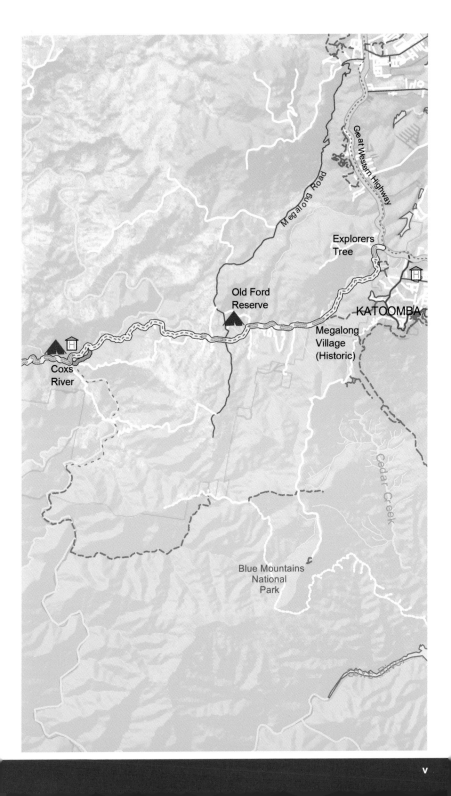

Introduction

The Six Foot Track is a not just a bushwalk but a historic journey – and a great adventure. Originally built about 2 metres wide, over 100 years ago, this route was quickly nicknamed the Six Foot (wide) Track. The name stuck, and now this walk takes you on a fantastic journey exploring the natural beauty and historic stories of this part of the Blue Mountains.

Starting from the Explorers Tree in Katoomba, the Six Foot Track was first established in 1884 to provide good access to Jenolan Caves by horse. Now revamped, this walk guides you through a mix of dense native bushland, past towering sandstone cliffs, granite creek beds, farmland, pine tree forests, and into the limestone valley of Jenolan.

Most people complete the Six Foot Track as a three-day hiking journey. The sense of achievement at the end of this historic walk is just fantastic, as is the chance to get away from it all and spend a few nights camping. You have the chance to share the track with a variety of Australian wildlife, such as wombats, kangaroos and wallabies, and a vast array of birds that you will see and hear along the way.

Whether you want to tackle the walk in one go, or split it into parts, this book provides notes and maps to help you plan your journey. You could try day walks, an overnight hike, an inn-to-inn luxury walk or join a tour group. The itineraries and information in the middle of the book will help you plan your walk at a pace that best suits you.

Early enthusiasts

Introduction

As with our other books, this book is not just about helping you on track, but helping you get excited and organised for your walk. You may find the book also becomes a bit of a souvenir. Walking the Six Foot Track makes you a part of history – you will want to share your journey with other people for many years to come.

Acknowledgements – from Matt McClelland

First I would like to acknowledge the traditional custodians of the land the Six Foot Track travels through, the Gundungurra and Wiradjuri peoples, and pay my respect to their elders both past and present.

Thank you also to the hardworking people at the Six Foot Track Heritage Trust, Crown Lands, NPWS, State Forests, Jenolan Caves Reserve Trust, and to the private land owners. So many people and different organisations work together to maintain this track and the surrounding environments and allow us passage.

Thank you to Kieran and Ian who first documented the Six Foot Track on www.wildwalks.com.

Geoff Mallinson and Caro Ryan have worked hard to produce the companion website for the book, www.sixfoottrack.com. Their expertise

in design and video production has been a wonderful asset. Their friendship and willingness to help carry the huge load of batteries on track is still an encouragement to me – thank you.

To the people at Woodslane, thanks for your continued commitment to quality. Thanks to Veechi Stuart who had the vision and kindly embraced this unusual upside-down book. Thanks to Kate Rowe the most helpful and thoughtful editor, she helped make this book not only legible but enjoyable to read. Thanks to Kasun Senaratne for the wonderful design effort, the book looks fantastic. Kasun also helped design the housing for the 360-degree camera system I built to take more than 10 000 panoramic images on the companion website. To my family and family in-law, thank you for your support and love. To my wife Fiona who is so kind as to encourage and work with me. And of course, to our two wonderful kids, Eric and Laura, thanks for the joy and fun times walking in the bush.

How to use this book

This book has been written to help you get the most out of your journey on the Six Foot Track. It has been a lot of fun writing it and we are sure you will have a lot of fun walking with it. This is our first 'upside-down book' that allows you to choose which direction you want to walk the track. You can start walking from either Katoomba or Jenolan Caves and both directions are equally good. In fact some people do both in one go, over two days – this is called the Twelve Foot Track!

Introduction

The tracknotes have been written in a visual way to help you read through and get a sense of the journey. This helps you prepare for the walk and also helps you visualise the walk better, so you will hardly need to pull the book out whilst walking.

There are three main parts to the book: the tracknotes from Katoomba to Jenolan, the reverse notes from Jenolan to Katoomba and, in the middle of this book, lots of extra helpful information to help in your planning, such as the history of the track, best times to walk, itineraries, tips, safety information, and lots more.

Exploring the tracks around Jenolan Caves

Walk grades and times

Establishing grades and times can be a little tricky, and there are many ways to classify a walk. The walks were initially graded using the AS 2156.1-2001, Australia's standard for track classification. To keep things simple, however, in this book each walk is classified Easy, Medium or Hard.

Some general rules of thumb when looking at walk grades in this book:

Easy: Mostly flat, suitable for all ages and for people new to bushwalking; take care with children. Generally good track surfaces. No bushwalking experience required. May include gentle hills or short section of steps.

Medium: Suitable for most ages and fitness levels, especially people who walk occasionally. May contain short, steeper sections, with loose, rough or sandy ground, or lots of steps. Sturdy shoes recommended.

Hard: Suitable for people who bushwalk regularly. Contains steep or rough sections, and/or requires particular attention to safety, navigation and bushcraft skills. Requires reasonable levels of fitness. Sturdy footwear essential.

For the walk as a whole, a good level of fitness is required. You'll soon figure out whether your own pace is faster or slower than is shown in this book. The walk times do not include time for rests, side trips or safety margins; please always allow extra time. In addition, remember that hills can really slow things down. A relatively flat six-kilometre walk will take half the time of a similar length walk that climbs and descends 600 metres (Google "Naismith's rule" to learn more). This has been taken into account for all the times provided in this book.

Introduction

Preparation and safety

This is a guide book; it is not a field guide or a bushcraft book. You will find a few hints and tips in this book, and an extensive Safety section, but it is not designed to give you survival, navigation or bushcraft skills. Please read the information about safety, facilities and other resources carefully, and think about what food, equipment and clothing you will carry, and also where you are going to collect water, and how you will treat it. The notes will not prompt you to collect water, as your need will vary greatly according to the season, weather and your supplies. However, you must make sure that you have always enough with you to supply you on the next leg of your journey.

The Six Foot Track is a wonderful walk, but it does lead into remote areas and therefore requires skills and knowledge for dealing with hazards. All the walks have significant possible hazards, such as potential flooding, hot weather, lighting strikes, sickness, food poisoning, tick bites, falls, bites, strains, etc. Many of these hazards are not specifically mentioned in this book, and even though they are unlikely to occur each walker needs to consider and manage any potential risk. A bit of time thinking and planning will help you have a safer and more enjoyable time.

Introduction

No journey is risk free; but the better prepared you are, the safer and more fun your journey is likely to be. Do spend time getting your body and mind ready. If you are not an experienced walker, start by reading and chatting with other people and exploring some smaller, easier walks. The book has been written to help you prepare, but there is so much that we can't cover — you will need to think through food, fitness, equipment, risks and skills. If you do not have the skills required, invite a friend with the skills, join a walking club or a tour or group, or undertake a course; there are always people happy to help you learn.

Maps

The following symbols are used in the maps for this book:

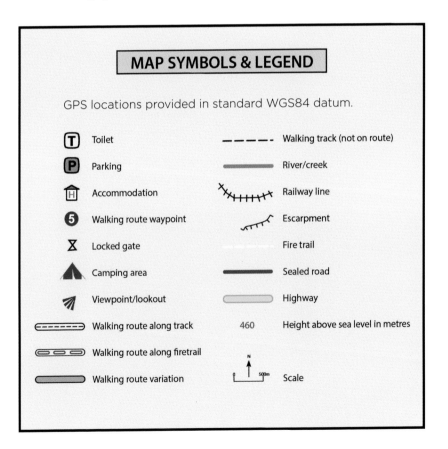

1 Jenolan Caves to Black Range Campsite

Beginning from the ancient and majestic Jenolan Caves, this walk will guide you through the southernmost section of the Six Foot Track. You start walking from the grand and historic Caves House, as you follow a series of narrow tracks through the native bushland out of the McKeown Valley before passing the Jenolan Caves Cottages and crossing Jenolan Caves Road. Keep an eye out for grazing kangaroos, wallabies – and, if you are lucky enough, some echidnas. You then walk along a series of undulating trails, through a few pleasant ferny forests then up onto the ridge, to finish at Black Range Campsite in the state forest. The spectacular Jenolan Caves provided the motivation to build the Six Foot Track more than a century ago, and the caves and the beautiful natural surroundings still draw in tourists from all around the world today.

At a glance

Grade: Medium/Hard

Time: 4 hrs 15 mins

Distance: 10.1 km one way

Ascent/descent: 720 metres ascent/330 metres descent

Conditions: Best avoided on very hot days. A few normally dry gullies that can get wet and muddy after rain. Steep loose rocky section near the start of the walk.

GPS of start: -33.8203, 150.0212

GPS of end: -33.7551, 150.0484

Getting there

Bus: Trolley Tours offers a $50 one-way deal from Katoomba to Jenolan. The bus leaves Katoomba at 9:30 am daily and takes about an hour and a half to get to Jenolan Caves. Tickets must be pre-booked and paid for by phoning 1800 801 577, or through their website: www.trolleytours.com.au. Trolley Tours can also often organise a special drop-off at waypoint 6, where the Six Foot Track crosses Jenolan Caves Road.

Car to Jenolan Caves: Follow Jenolan Caves Road from the Great Western Highway (about 11 kilometres west of Mount Victoria) for 46 kilometres. The caves are well signposted along the road. Once through the Grand Arch you will pass Caves House (on your left). There is free parking further along the road. The last section of this road is one-way, heading into the valley from 11:45 am to 1:15 pm every day (to allow for buses). If you want to drive out during this time you will need to go via Oberon.

Car to Black Range Campsite: From the Great Western Highway about 11 kilometres west of Mount Victoria, turn onto Jenolan Caves Road following the Jenolan Caves sign. Stay on Jenolan Caves Road for 23.6 kilometres, passing through Hampton, and continue straight ahead at the intersection with Duckmaloi Road (where there are traffic lights and road closed boom gates). Keep following the signs to Jenolan Caves for

another 8.8 kilometres to the signposted intersection with Boggy Creek Road (a dirt road on your right). Turn left here and follow the dirt road (it initially veers a little left) as it leads into the pine forest for 1.2 kilometres (passing a few side roads) to come to a large intersection. Turn left and then almost immediately right, following the *Six Foot Track Black Range Camping Ground* sign. Follow the dirt road for about 100 metres until you come to the signposted and fenced Black Range Campsite, on your right.

If you are driving from Jenolan Caves House, drive through the Grand Arch and continue along Jenolan Caves Road for 11 kilometres to where the Six Foot Track crosses the road marked with a yellow walker sign. Continue along the road for just over 2.5 kilometres and turn right onto the dirt (2WD) road (opposite the signposted Boggy Creek Road). Follow the dirt road (it initially veers a little left) and into the pine forest for 1.2 kilometres (passing a few side roads) to come to a large intersection. Turn left and then almost immediately right, following the *Six Foot Track - Black Range Camping Ground* sign. Follow the dirt road for about 100 metres until you come to the signposted and fenced Black Range Campsite, on your right.

Jenolan Caves to Black Range Campsite

Point of interest – Jenolan Caves & Jenolan Caves House

No walk on the Six Foot Track is complete without seeing some of the spectacular underground scenery at Jenolan Caves – after all, the track was built to allow access to these majestic places. Give yourself some extra time to join a guided or self-guided cave tour. These spectacular limestone caves have been a popular tourist destination since the late 19th century. There are daily tours and activities – you will need to book into a tour to gain access to most of the caves. Call 1300 763 311 for more information. If you are short on time, make sure you walk through the Grand Arch and have a quick explore of the limestone formations. You can squeeze in one of the early tours before you start your walk, or better still come down the day before and give yourself time to enjoy the larger cave tours.

Jenolan Caves House, built in 1898, is a heritage-listed building with a variety of accommodation options and other services for visitors to the caves. Jenolan has two licensed restaurants: Trails Bistro is open from breakfast onwards and closes early evening, and serves a range of light meals including sandwiches, salads and hot food; Chisholm's Restaurant is open each morning for breakfast and each evening for dinner from 6 pm. Essential items and souvenirs may be purchased from Things Jenolan, located on the ground floor of Caves House. For more information, call Jenolan Caves on 1300 763 311. Accommodation ranges from $70-$500 per night for two people, from bunk house to premium rooms with ensuite.

Walk directions

1 From the seat directly opposite the main entrance to Caves House (on the other side of the road), follow the *Six Foot Track* sign up the concrete steps. Follow the stone footpath up the side of the valley for about 80 metres to pass the *Southside Show Caves* information sign, then just over 30 metres later the *Grand Arch* information sign and view of the arch. Continue fairly gently up the path for 100 metres (as it bends right) to find a *Caves House* information sign and some great views back to where you started from. The going gets steeper now: the path begins to zigzag up past a seat and more views down to Caves House for 150 metres, passing beside the limestone cliffs. At the top of this climb the path leads over a small rise then gently down to a fenced lookout beside Carlotta Arch, a large and spectacular cave remnant overlooking Blue Lake. It is believed that the arch was named in honour of a daughter of the surveyor General P. F. Adams who is credited with having taken some of the earliest photos at Jenolan.

2 Continue straight ahead, following the gravel path past the top of the steps and gently uphill

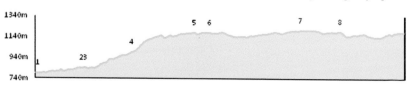

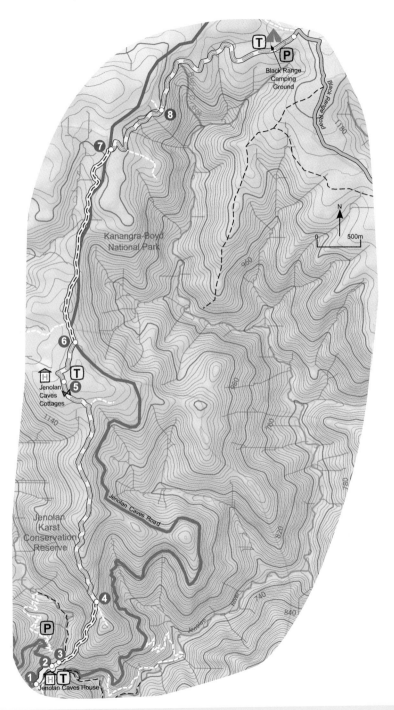

Australian fauna – Animals around Jenolan Caves

The area around Jenolan Caves is home to a wide variety of Australian native animals and birds. Platypuses can be seen in Blue Lake most days at dawn and dusk, and there are eastern water dragons in the river. There are lots of wombats, wallabies (in the car park!), rosellas, yellow-breasted robins and willy wagtails. And the brush-tailed rock wallaby is making a return to Jenolan, thanks to a weed control program which is restoring native habitat in the area.

Further along this section of the Six Foot Track, there are yellow-tailed black cockatoos enjoying themselves in the pine forest. Along the track you may also see echidnas, and even snakes – for more information about the red-bellied black snake, Turn this book over and go to page 37.

a short distance to an intersection with a *Six Foot Track* signpost.

3 Turn right to follow the *Six Foot Track* sign up along the track, which will soon lead you up some steep timber steps. After about 50 metres you come to the top of a narrow limestone ridge with beautiful views down to Blue Lake on your right. Platypus can be spotted in this lake, though perhaps not from this height! The track leads you across the narrow saddle then uphill along the side of the McKeown Valley for 300 metres, passing under a solid, leaning gum tree. The track continues uphill, steeply in parts, and crosses a few gullies for 500 metres. You will then pass between two timber posts with the Mount George trail.

4 Veer left and walk uphill, following the particularly steep rocky trail.

The trail continues steeply for about 600 metres, then eases off a little for another 400 metres and begins to follow the top of the ridge line, more or less. The trail continues to lead you generally uphill for another 1.5 kilometres to pass a mostly flat clearing. Continue along the trail, gently uphill, for another 300 metres and turn left at an intersection marked with a *Kia-ora Hill Fire Trail* sign. Head along this mostly flat trail for 350 metres, through the tall wooded forest and on to a metal gate. After walking around the gate and straight ahead down the driveway for about 60 metres you pass beside the Jenolan Caves Cottages. (For more information about Jenolan Caves Cottages, Turn this book over and go to page 40.)

5 Continue straight past the cottages, following the driveway gently down-

hill past the clearing. The gravel driveway soon bends right and leads you up past a toilet block on your right. Continue up along the driveway for about 350 metres and head over a small rise, then down to an intersection a few metres before the sealed Jenolan Caves Road.

6 Veer left at the intersection, following the 6FT arrow post along the track and keeping the road a short distance to your right. After about 150 metres you will follow another gravel driveway, leaving the road to walk around the edge of a re-vegetating clearing. Here the track widens and leads up over a pleasantly wooded hill for about 600 metres, passing a 40 kilometres 6FT arrow, and arrives back down near the road again. Follow the track fairly close to the road and powerlines for 400 metres to a large blue *Jenolan Caves Welcome* sign

Carlotta Arch

1 Jenolan Caves to Black Range Campsite

(facing away), where the track narrows.

Soon, you will head downhill for about 130 metres to cross a ferny gully then climb up some timber steps. At the top of these steps turn left, and follow the mostly flat track around the side of a small hill for 40 metres before turning left again a bit before the road. The track leads down more welcome timber steps for about 40 metres, crossing another similar gully with tall eucalypt trees on a small, flat timber plank bridge. Climb up a series of timber steps for about 80 metres and turn left at the 6FT arrow post. Now

the track leads you around another small hill for 120 metres, arriving beside the road. Walk behind the safety rail for about 30 metres before heading around the side of another small hill for 200 metres. From here walk down timber steps for 100 metres before crossing yet another pleasant ferny and tree-filled gully on a small, flat timber plank bridge and climbing up more timber steps. Turn left again and follow the 6FT arrow post as the track meanders along the side of the hill for about 300 metres to pass a *Road Ahead* sign, and arrives at the edge of the sealed Jenolan Caves Road. This

time you cross the road – taking care with traffic – to the large clearing and gravel stockpile on the other side.

7 Veer left at the gravel stockpile and follow the 6FT arrow post along the wide dirt trail. After about 20 metres the trail leads you past a *Road Ahead* sign (facing away), then bends right about 90 metres later at a large grassy clearing. Continue along the trail for another 120 metres to an intersection with another trail, which is marked with a 6FT arrow post pointing left.

Veer left, following the 6FT arrow post gently downhill along the clear trail, and along the side of the hill for 300 metres to a pleasant gully. Continue fairly steeply uphill for about 250 metres to a bend, then after 50 metres you will come to an intersection with another trail on your left.

8 Continue straight on, following the 6FT arrow post along the wide trail which soon leads you steeply downhill, past a few out of place Telstra posts, for about 250 metres. Here the trail becomes less steep for just shy of 300 metres, coming to a Y-intersection with a faint trail on your left. Take the right fork, staying on

the main trail, and wander uphill through tall open eucalypt forest, with a ferny understorey which is home to many birds. After about 250 metres you arrive at a clearing at the top of the ridge. The trail bends left and leads more gently downhill for 500 metres past a few 6FT arrow posts, then bends right to cross a ferny gully, the upper reaches of Bulls Creek. You then continue uphill for 600 metres to pass a 35 km 6FT arrow post. After another 200 metres of walking up through the tall wooded forest, you come to an intersection with another trail (on your right), in view of Black Range Camping Ground, which means you are almost there.

Continue straight ahead, and follow the 6FT arrow post gently uphill along the main dirt road, which leads along the edge of the campsite for about 100 metres, then walk around the green metal gate to find the information sign in front of the Black Range Camping Ground on your left. (To continue along the Six Foot Track, head straight on, following the next set of notes: **Black Range Campsite to Coxs River Campsite**.)

Point of interest – Black Range camping ground

Black Range camping ground is a fenced campsite beside the Six Foot Track, and is also accessible by car. The well-maintained and signposted campsite has a couple of sheltered picnic tables, toilets, rainwater tank and an information board with map. The campsite is in a large fenced grassy area, with a stand of native trees. In the evening and early mornings you may find a few of the local wallabies grazing around the campgrounds. The tank water is quite reliable but the tank can become empty during long dry spells or through vandalism; please treat before use. A sign reminds campers that this is a Fuel Stove Only area – no camp fires.

2 Black Range Campsite to Coxs River Campsite

Following in the historic footsteps of generations before, this walk guides you through the middle section of the Six Foot Track. You have the chance to explore a wide variety of bushland, from the dry open forests high on the ridge lines through farmland to the moist tree fern gullies of Little River. Walking along a well-managed 4WD dirt road and crossing a few creeks, you will descend from 1200 m above sea level to 290 m and the edge of the Coxs River. There are some beautiful views towards the Katoomba escarpment from Kiangatha Yards. The valley at Alum Creek and Little River provides a pleasant cool spot to rest or camp. Finishing at the Coxs River is a real treat as you can take a dip and explore the holes carved in the granite riverbed or just wander among the casuarina stands beside the water.

At a glance

Grade: Hard

Time: 7 hrs 30 mins

Distance: 19 km one way

Ascent/descent: 400 metres ascent/1310 metres descent

Conditions: Following a 4WD dirt road for the whole walk, little shade; best avoided on hot days. A lot of downhill walking, steep in places; can be hard on your knees. Some creek crossing where you are likely to get wet feet; creeks may become impassable after rain.

GPS of start: -33.7551, 150.0484
GPS of end: -33.7433, 150.1787

Fire trail near Kiangatha Yards

Getting there

Car: From the Great Western Hwy about 11 kilometres west of Mount Victoria, turn onto Jenolan Caves Road following the Jenolan Caves sign. Stay on Jenolan Caves Road for 23.6 kilometres (passing through Hampton) and continue straight ahead at the intersection with Duckmaloi Rd, where there are traffic lights and road closed boom gates. Keep following the signs to Jenolan Caves for another 8.8 kilometres to pass

Boggy Creek Road (a dirt road on your right). After 450 metres further along the main sealed Jenolan Caves Road you will come to an intersection with unsignposted Black Range Road, a dirt road on your left. Turn left onto this dirt (2WD) road, then after 860 metres turn right at the large 5-way intersection. After just 100 metres you will come to the signposted and fenced Black Range Campsite, on your right.

Drive to Coxs River Campsite: Car access is possible in a 4WD to the Coxs River Campsite. This walk follows the 4WD road all the way, so to drive to the Coxs River just follow the notes for this walk in a 4WD. At times this can be a challenging drive and some four wheel driving experience is recommended.

The well-maintained Black Range camping ground is a fenced campsite beside the Six Foot Track, and is also accessible by car. For more information, refer to the box in the previous walk on page 15.

Australian birds – Yellow-tailed black cockatoos

The eastern yellow-tailed black cockatoo (*Calyptorhynchus funereus*) is found in many areas on the east coast of Australia and you are fairly likely to see them flying over your heads on the Six Foot Track. These birds are about 60 centimetres long and are covered mostly in dark, brownish-black feathers with a short crest on their head. The birds have distinct yellow cheek feathers and a wide yellow band on the tail feathers, which is visible in flight. These cockatoos lay their eggs at the end of the year in nests built in vertical tree hollows. After about a month the eggs hatch and the birds tend to stay with their parents for about a year. The birds enjoy eating seeds from the eucalypts and the she-oaks so keep an eye out along the banks of the Coxs River and on Black Range for these magnificent birds.

2 Black Range Campsite to Coxs River Campsite

Walk directions

1 From the information sign in front of Black Range Camping Ground, follow the dirt road gently uphill, initially keeping the campsite to your left. (For more information about Black Range camping ground refer to the previous walk on page 15.)

After about 100 metres you pass under some powerlines, then come to a clear, large, 5-way intersection marked with a *Six Foot Track – Black Range Camping Ground* sign pointing back down the road.

2 Turn right and follow the *Six Foot Track* sign uphill along the dirt road, keeping the pine forest to your left. After about

250 metres you come to a clear 3-way intersection marked with a *6't metal arrow post* (on your left).

3 Turn right and walk downhill, away from the pine forest and towards the powerlines along the dirt road. The dirt road soon bends left and follows near the powerlines again for about 400 metres, where the road straightens out and continues downhill past an intersection with another trail (on your left), just at the edge of the clearing. About 25 metres later the road leads past the *Black Range Fire Trail* sign and continues for another 80 metres to a Y-intersection with a faint trail on the right.

4 Continue straight ahead, following the 6FT arrow post gently downhill along the wide, dirt Black Range Road. After about 500 metres you walk past a short trail on your left (it leads into a clearing that has been used as a campsite). Continue along the main road as it gently undulates along the top of the ridge for 1.2 kilometres and passes an intersection marked with a metal *Kanangra Boyd National Park* sign. About 400 metres later the road leads you down a short steep section, and soon arrives at an intersection with the signposted Beefsteak Creek Fire Trail on your left.

Ignore this fire trail and continue straight ahead,

gently downhill, along the main dirt road. After almost 400 metres the road splits in two for a short distance. Continue for another 100 metres to an intersection with signposted Warlock Fire Trail (on your right).

5 Continue straight on, following the 6`t arrow on a metal post downhill on Black Range Road. After about 900 metres this road leads you down another short steep section then continues to guide you along the top of the ridge line, gently undulating through the pleasant open forest for 2.3 kilometres to pass a small dam on the side of the road. Although we at Wildwalks are yet to see any, one walker told us they saw a koala along this section –

so keep an eye out. You are more likely to spot some glossy yellow-tailed black cockatoos. About 100 metres past this small dam you come to an intersection with Moorara Boss Fire Trail (on your right).

6 Continue straight ahead, still following the 6`t arrow on a metal post downhill along Black Range Road. The dirt road continues to undulate along the top of the ridge line through the pleasant forest and past a few large ant mounds for 2.1 kilometres, moderately steeply downhill in a few places, until coming to a clearing at an intersection with the signposted Cronje Mountain Fire Trail.

7 This is where the real downhill section starts.

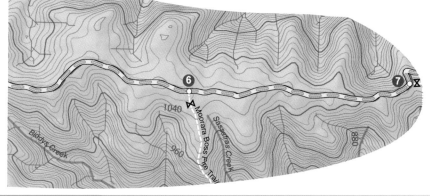

2 Black Range Campsite to Coxs River Campsite

Veer left, following the 6`t metal arrow post along the dirt road steeply downhill. After just shy of 150 metres the dirt road leads around a right-hand hairpin bend to find some views of the distant escarpment. The road continues to wind fairly steeply downhill for another 700 metres to pass a clearing on the top of the ridge (on your right). Here the road bends left and leads downhill for another 150 metres, passing a 25 *km* 6FT arrow post. After 400 metres you will arrive at an intersection with the signposted Waterfall Creek Fire Trail (on your left).

8 Turn right and follow the arrow on the metal post, fairly steeply downhill, continuing down along the dirt Glen Chee Road. The road soon leads past a *Drive with Caution Walkers On Road* sign, then after

about 800 metres you pass another large flat clearing on your right. About 150 metres further downhill, the road leads around a right-hand hairpin

bend then continues fairly steeply downhill for another 500 metres, where it bends fairly sharply right again at the site of the old Kiangatha gates. Continue downhill along the dirt road which soon leads around a sharp left bend, and continues down through a narrow gully for another 300 metres to come to the edge of Little River.

Walk across the usually shallow

Little River, enjoying the tree ferns, the mossy valley and the water running between your toes. You will need to cross the river again, 110 metres further along the road, and cross it once more after another 110 metres. Now continue along the road for another 300 metres,

become impassable after heavy or prolonged rain, or may completely dry up in dry weather. Just shy of 100 metres further along, the road bends right to lead up to the signposted and gated Alum Creek Reserve and camping area on your left.

metres to the intersection at the other end of the regenerating trail. Continue up along the dirt road for another 40 metres, where it bends right around the edge of a grassy clearing. After this the road continues up, moderately steeply in places, for

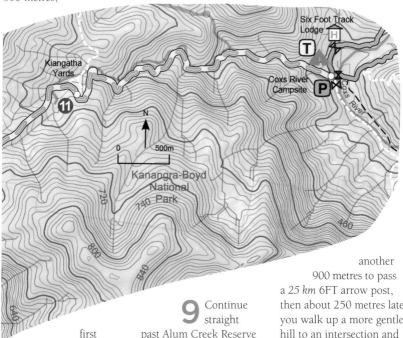

first beside the river then through old farmland, to pass a *Drive with Caution Walker on Road* sign. Over the next 300 metres this dirt road leads through more old farmland, passes between two timber posts, then dips down to cross Alum Creek, which is also usually shallow. Both Little River and Alum Creek may

9 Continue straight past Alum Creek Reserve campsite and toilet, following the dirt Glen Chee Road uphill. The road leads moderately steeply uphill for just over 350 metres to an intersection with a regenerating trail where you turn right. The dirt road then leads you through a dip, then steeply uphill for just shy of 300

another 900 metres to pass a *25 km* 6FT arrow post, then about 250 metres later you walk up a more gentle hill to an intersection and Mini Mini Saddle clearing.

10 Veer left, staying on the main dirt road as it leads steeply downhill off the side of the ridge. After about 300 metres the road flattens out for a short time, at a grassy clearing with views of the distant escarpment. It then continues, noticeably

Point of interest – Alum Creek Camping Ground

Signposted as Alum Creek Reserve, this flat grassy area, off the side of the dirt Glen Chee Road, is the 'extra' campsite on the Six Foot Track. The campsite is the least used and least developed of the three official campsites on the Six Foot Track, and makes a good place to stay if attempting the walk in two days, as it sits close to the middle of the full Six Foot Track. There is a pit toilet near the entrance and you will find the flat, green campsite is in a well-protected valley, surrounded by trees, with the small Alum Creek beside it and the fairly reliable Little River down the road (treat water before use).

downhill, for another 700 metres to pass a *Grid* sign and then crosses a cattle grid. Over the next 250 metres the road bends right then passes two *Grid* signs (facing away). Continue along the dirt road for another 250 metres and pass straight through an intersection towards the cattle grid and *No Through Road Locked Gate* sign beside Kiangatha Cattle Yards (on your left).

11 Continue straight to carefully cross the cattle grid, open the gate on the main road (chain on the right) and pass through (closing the gate again) and then head gently uphill between the 4x4 vehicles only sign for about 150 metres. You then proceed down along the side of the hill for almost 200 metres, and

pass another *Drive With Caution Walkers on Road* sign. There are some great views here across the Coxs River valley to the escarpment near Katoomba. Keep following the dirt Glen Chee Road as it leads you around a sharp right bend then winds moderately steeply downhill for about 2.1 kilometres and crosses Gibraltar Creek, which is usually shallow.

Woodland near Mini Mini Saddle

2 Black Range Campsite to Coxs River Campsite

You then continue more gently down under the high-tension powerlines to cross another usually small creek, then continue generally downhill for 200 metres to pass close to the high-tension powerline tower (up the hill to your right). After another 150 metres you will cross Gibraltar Creek again – this creek may become impassable after heavy or prolonged rain, or can also often dry up in dry weather.

Continue along the road for another 150 metres gently uphill to the turning circle and locked gate at the top of the campsite. Walk through the gap beside the fence and either through the Coxs River Campsite or along the trail beside to a clear intersection (about 40 metres before the Coxs River) marked with a *Six Foot Track* sign.

(To continue along the Six Foot Track, either walk straight ahead to cross the Coxs River, following the alternate route notes in the next section, OR turn left and follow the main notes to use the Swing Bridge crossing.

Both sets of notes are found in the next walk: **Coxs River to Megalong Valley.**)

Coxs River crossing in flood

2 Black Range Campsite to Coxs River Campsite

Point of interest – Coxs River Campsite

Coxs River Campsite, on the Six Foot Track, is found on the western bank of the Coxs River. You will find a sheltered picnic table, water (rain tank or creek – treat before drinking either), toilet and a flat, grassed camping area with excellent access to the river. This campsite is all about the river: spend some time on the bank enjoying the clear evening air, surrounded by the high ridge lines as the water continues to carve its way through the granite and sandy riverbed. (Be very careful if deciding to swim as it can be very dangerous after rain.)

The campsite is used by people walking the Six Foot Track, but is also visited at times by people who have driven in using their 4WD. It is a pleasant place to camp, especially on warmer days with the river as a great place to cool down. Be very careful if deciding to swim as it can be very dangerous after rain.

You're likely to be able to spot possums and other wildlife at night at this campsite (and indeed, at all of the campsites along the track).

For information on how to spot possums and other wildlife at night please, turn this book over and go to page 33.

3 Coxs River Campsite to Megalong Valley

Starting beside the Coxs River, this section of the Six Foot Track explores a mix of farmland and native forest on its climb up the Megalong Road. In this section you can enjoy the cool waters of the river and the many cascades carved from the granite rock bed. Leaving the valley you have the choice of wading across the river, or bringing out your inner adventurer on the memorable Bowtells metal swing bridge above. You will then climb up the side of the hill through dry bushland, reaching open farmlands and pockets of forest, and later you will have a chance to explore the historic Megalong Cemetery. The dirt road at the start of this walk is 4WD access only from Jenolan Caves Rd, making the walk best done as part of the overall weekend Six Foot Track hike.

At a glance

Grade: Medium

Time: 3 hrs 30 mins

Distance: 7.5 km one way

Ascent/descent: 610 metres ascent/310 metres descent

Conditions: All the significant waterway crossings are bridged. Best to avoid on very hot days, although on warm days you can make the most of the Coxs River.

GPS of start: -33.7433, 150.1787

GPS of end: -33.7356, 150.2346

Bowtells Swing Bridge

3 Coxs River Campsite to Megalong Valley

Getting there

Car: If doing this as a day walk, it will usually be easier to allow extra time and do this walk following the reverse notes in Megalong Valley to Coxs River campsite (page 16), then retrace your steps back to your car. Car access is possible in a 4WD to the Coxs River Campsite. Follow the tracknotes for the Black Range to Coxs River campsite walk, as that walk follows the road all the way. At times this can be a challenging drive and some four wheel driving experience is recommended.

Driving to the Megalong Road Trackhead: From Blackheath, cross the train line then turn left to follow Station St, then right onto Shipley Rd and left onto Megalong Road. Now drive along Megalong Road for just over 14 kilometres. Soon after you cross Megalong Creek you will find a well-signposted parking area where the Six Foot Track crosses the road. (If the main road becomes dirt you have gone too far.)

Walk variation – Six Foot Track route crossing the Coxs River

From waypoint 1, from the intersection just south of the Coxs River Campsite, follow the *Six Foot Track* sign downhill for about 40 metres to the sandy beach on the bank of the river. Please heed the *Do Not Cross River When In Flood Use Alternative Bridge* warning sign, as this river is normally about shin-deep in the rocky section – if it is deeper, or the water is moving fast, consider using the swing bridge upstream. Cross the river at the beach in the deeper sandy section, or in the shallower section where the river may flow in two or three sections across smooth and slippery rocks.

On the far side you will find a large clearing on the floodplain. Walk across the floodplain then moderately steeply up a short hill to the *Six Foot Track* sign. Turn left to walk up along the trail beside a timber fence for about 70 metres to an intersection (where the trail bends right). Continue straight along the clear but narrower track for about 800 metres, crossing several gullies along the side of the hill, to an intersection with a track just before the swing bridge. Continue along the upper track for another 30 metres to a signposted intersection, above the bridge where a *Six Foot Track* sign points back along the track. Now continue straight to stay on the Six Foot Track, following the notes from waypoint 4.

3 Coxs River Campsite to Megalong Valley

Walk directions

1 From the lower side of the camping area, follow the *Six Foot Track Bridge Crossing* sign along the wide trail, initially keeping the main camping area to your left and the Coxs River to your right. (For more information about Coxs River Campsite, refer to page 25 for the previous walk.) Continue along this trail for another 230 metres as it leads up to an intersection with a track (on your right) just before a locked private property gate.

Veer right, following the *Six Foot Track* sign down along the clear track. The track leads down for almost 50 metres where you climb a fence using a stile. Follow the track across a small gully and walk a short distance to an intersection with the timber path (on your left), below the Six Foot Track Lodge.

2 Continue straight, passing below the Six Foot Track Lodge, following the mostly flat track along the side of the hill for about 70 metres where you walk through a gate with a *Welcome* sign. Continue along the side of the hill for just over 100 metres, where the track bends right and you walk down a set of timber steps to an intersection and clearing marked with a *Private Land – No Camping* sign.

Turn sharp left at this pleasant open clearing and walk up the timber steps. As you walk up you enter the drier forest and, as the views down to the river begin to open up, the sounds of whipbirds and the water in the river get you excited for the upcoming bridge crossing. At the top of this rise the track leads between a couple of fence posts and you continue

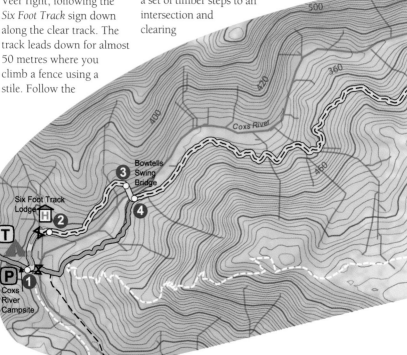

3 Coxs River Campsite to Megalong Valley

along the side of the hill for another 500 metres, crossing a few gullies and climbing up and down a series of timber steps. The track now bends right and leads you down another set of steps through dense vegetation, past the *Bowtells Bridge* sign, to a rock platform on the north side of the bridge, with great views over the Coxs River.

3 Step up onto the suspension bridge and cross the Coxs River, observing the

Only one person at a time safety sign. This crossing can take some time with a large group – the bridge may swing a fair bit and people concerned by heights may find this challenging. The bridge spans 100 metres, giving amazing views of the river below. On the far side, a ramp leads to a clearing. (If you want you can scramble down over the slippery boulders to the river from here.) As you step off the

bridge veer left, walking up the timber steps for about 20 metres to the main track, where you will find a few *Six Foot Track* signs.

4 Turn left to walk fairly gently uphill along the track, keeping the valley and river down to your left. After about 150 metres you will walk through a pleasant, lush gully with views close to the river, where you can keep your

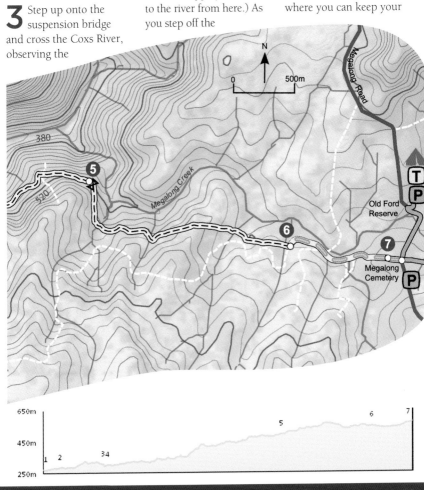

Bowtells Swing Bridge

eye out for dancing willy wagtails between the casuarinas. You then head up two sets of timber steps and walk along the side of the valley for about 1 kilometre, leaving the main view of the Coxs River behind. The track bends right into a gully with some large granite boulders – one of the boulders (on your right) has a small overhang, home to a wild beehive. Here the track bends left to cross the gully, then heads up a 100-metre-long series of timber steps, followed by a gentle uphill section for 400 metres, a short set of timber steps beside granite boulders, and a 250-metre uphill section, until you pass through a gate, which is usually closed.

Continue more gently up along the side of the valley for another 600 metres to an intersection with a wide trail. Turn right then immediately left as the track narrows again, and continue for just over 200 metres to cross a timber fence on a metal stile. About 120 metres further along this track, you will find another closed gate marked with a few *Private Property* signs.

5 Continue straight ahead, walking through the gate (and closing it behind you) and heading uphill along the track. Remember to stay on the track, as this section passes through private property. Continue for about 600 metres through a mix of farmland and open forest, crossing a few steep gullies with timber steps before climbing over a fence using a metal stile. About 150 metres further on, you pass a 10 km 6FT arrow post. The track winds along the side of the hill for 100 metres, crosses another steep gully, and climbs up some timber steps into more open farmland, then winds along the side of the grassy hill for 150 metres, passing a *Private Land - No Camping before Coxs River Reserve* sign (looking away from you).

You then wander downhill for 200 metres and cross a fence using a metal stile beside a large tree, then continue for 300 metres over a series of hills through the open farmland before crossing another fence with a stile. The track turns left here, and you will follow a fence across a valley, above a dam, for almost 100 metres, then over a rise and down some timber steps, with great views to the escarpment. Cross a small creek on the timber Guyver Bridge – the bridge is named in honour of Jon Guyver, who worked hard to redevelop the Six Foot Track as the track co-ordinator/administrator until 2010. Now it is just a short uphill walk to a T-intersection with a private dirt road beside a cattle grid.

6 Turn left to follow the dirt road over the cattle grid and gently downhill for just over 200 metres, towards the view of the escarpment, then cross

Point of interest – Bowtells Swing Bridge

This suspension footbridge spans the Coxs River and provides an alternate route for the Six Foot Track when the river is in flood. Regardless of weather, this route is now becoming more popular, with many walkers wanting to avoid the river crossing and enjoy this exciting experience, and the unique view. The bridge was built and opened in 1992 by the Royal Australian Engineers. The bridge is named after a fellow soldier of the builders, Corporal Bob Bowtell, who died whilst attempting to clear a tunnel of the VC during the Vietnam war. Bowtell grew up in Katoomba and was buried in West Malaysia.

3 Coxs River Campsite to Megalong Valley

another cattle grid. Keep following the dirt road for about 50 metres, passing a few intersections and passing close by Megalong Creek, where a sign reminds walkers that they are on private land. Continue straight on, walking uphill along the dirt road for another 150 metres to cross yet another cattle grid. Then, just shy of 300 metres later, after passing a few driveways and walking beside more farmland,

Point of interest – Six Foot Track Lodge

The Six Foot Track Lodge sits above the flats of the Coxs River, not far north of Coxs River Campsite. The architect-designed lodge has two cabins, each of which can sleep 12 people in bunks. Each cabin has warm blankets, pillows, log fire, pizza oven, tank water and its own outhouse toilet. At $40 per person per night, and surrounded by beautiful trees, animals and birds, this is a very pleasant way to spend an evening. Meal packs can also be organised for a fee. For more information, visit www.sixfoottrackecolodge.com, or call/text Lucie 0431 072 862. All bookings must be made before starting your walk – the cabin is not staffed and is locked. Campsite near the Coxs River available for $25 pp, with campfires allowed.

3 Coxs River Campsite to Megalong Valley

this road leads through a gate with a *No Through Road* sign (facing away). Continue heading uphill along the road through the tranquil forest for 80 metres to a stone memorial on your right, marking Megalong Cemetery. (For more information about the cemetery, turn this book over and go to page 17.)

7 Continue past the Megalong Cemetery, along the dirt road for another 80 metres to a clearing and a large sheltered *Six Foot Track* information sign. Either cross over the cattle grid or stile to the car park beside the sealed Megalong Road.

(To continue the Six Foot Track, cross the road and continue straight, following the notes in walk 4: **Megalong Valley to Explorers Tree**.)

GUYVER BRIDGE

Walk variation – Alternate Route to access Old Ford Reserve campsite

From the end of this walk, turn left to follow the Old Ford Reserve Picnic & Camping Ground 500 metres sign gently downhill along the sealed Megalong Road. After about 360 metres the road bends left then leads down to cross Megalong Creek on the raised concrete ford. This creek does flood at times and can become unsafe to cross. Just after crossing the creek, veer right into the large car-based camping area.

Old Ford Reserve campsite is on the northern bank of Megalong Creek. The campsite is accessible by car, has a wheelchair-accessible toilet, and plenty of flat space to pitch a tent. You may spot a wombat or eastern grey kangaroo here and the nice groupings of trees and access to the creek make this a pleasant enough place to stay. (For more about wombats, turn this book over and go to page 20.) Being on the side of the road this campsite does attract some loud campers at times.

4 Megalong Valley to Explorers Tree

This walk guides you along the easternmost section of the Six Foot Track and the final leg if you are doing this as a through walk. Starting from the Megalong Road Trackhead, you will then spend much of your time looking up to the grand views of the ever-approaching escarpment as you wind through a mix of remote farmland and native bushland. Soon after passing the historic Megalong Village site, you will head up Nellies Glen – a steep climb through a beautiful and moist canyon. At the top of Nellies Glen is a worthwhile short side trip to Norths Lookout, with spectacular views down across the valley you have just walked up. From here it is a fairly short walk up to the historic Explorers Tree and the end of the Six Foot Track.

At a glance

Grade: Hard

Time: 3 hrs 45 mins

Distance: 8.2 km one way

Ascent/descent: 600 metres ascent/120 metres descent

Conditions: The walk up through Nellies Glen is steep and can be slippery. There are a couple of creeks that can become impassable after heavy or prolonged rain.

GPS of start: -33.7356, 150.2346

GPS of end: -33.704, 150.2913

Getting there

Car: From Blackheath cross the train line then turn left to follow Station St. Turn right onto Shipley Rd and left onto Megalong Road, then drive along Megalong Road for just over 14 kilometres. Soon after crossing Megalong Creek you will find a well-signposted parking area where the Six Foot Track crosses the road. (If the main road becomes dirt you have gone too far.)

If you are planning a day walk you will need to organise a car shuffle. To access the end of this walk, drive west along the Great Western Hwy from Parke St (the main road into Katoomba) for just over 2 kilometres, then turn left into the signposted Nellies Glen Rd at the Explorers Tree. There is a dirt parking area on the left about 60 metres from the highway.

Walk directions

1 From the car park on Megalong Road, head east following the *Six Foot Track* sign across the sealed road (away from cattle grid and information signs) to climb over a fence using a stile. A sign reminds walkers to stay on the track as this section is on private property. Now follow a narrow track through the bush for just over 200 metres and then continue straight at a 4-way inter-section. About 150 metres later you cross Mclennan Bridge, named after Mr Michael (Mick) Mclellan who has been in charge of the maintenance of the Six Foot Track for many years. Continue through the fairly dense forest for another 300 metres where you cross another fence using a stile to find a wider trail in more open farmland. Turn left and follow the

trail over a rise, through the farmland with a nice view of the escarpment, for another 300 metres, then cross Mitchells Creek – this creek may become impassable after heavy or prolonged rain. Now veer a little left and walk through the open grassland for 130 metres, passing a *Private Land No Camping* sign, to

climb over a fence using a stile. Here you come to an intersection marked with a *Six Foot Track* sign beside the dirt Nellies Glen Road, with the pleasant Megalong Creek ford on your left.

2 Continue straight, and follow the *Six Foot Track* sign gently uphill along the dirt Nellies Glen

4 Megalong Valley to Explorers Tree

Road for about 300 metres, passing a large *Road subject to flooding* sign (facing away) and then heading below a nearby house. About 120 metres later, the road leaves the powerlines and continues through the remote farmland valley for another 900 metres, passing a series of drive-ways, before coming to the locked Wari-Wari gate. Veer a little to the left to climb over the fence using the stile, then continue along the Nellies Glen trail for about 170 metres to the 3-way intersection marked with a *Six Foot Track* sign.

3 Veer left, following the *Six Foot Track* sign north-east along the wide Nellies Glen trail, which soon crosses the usually small Corral Creek. Here the trail tends east for just

shy of 400 metres to lead you past a *5 km* 6FT arrow post. Continue towards the view of the escarpment, through the tall scribbly gum forest, for another 500 metres. You will cross another usually small creek, and then head through a gate, which is usually closed. Keep following the trail for another 250 metres to find the signposted old Megalong Village site on your right, which is now a horse paddock.

4 Continue straight past the old Megalong Village site, following the wide Nellies Glen trail. The trail almost immediately heads over the

culverted Diamond Creek – another pleasant spot to cool down on a hot day – to find an intersection marked with a *Six Foot Track* sign and the Devils Hole trail on your right. Continue straight ahead, following the *Six Foot Track* sign gently uphill along the main wide trail for another 500 metres to cross the culverted Devils Hole Creek, just after an unused concrete pipe with wild beehives inside. The trail continues generally uphill through the scribbly gum forest for about 1.4 kilometres to a small

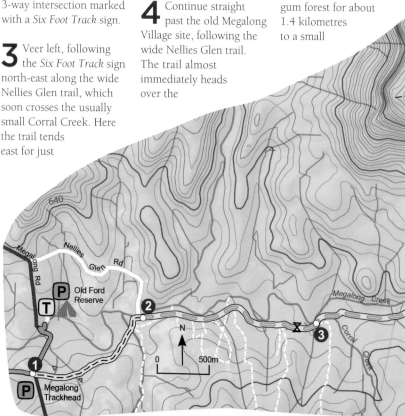

clearing and turning area at the end of the trail, where you will see a narrower track just a bit to the right. (For more information

about scribbly gum trees, and how their markings are formed, please turn this book over and refer to the box on page 14.)

5 Veer right to follow the clear but narrower track down and across a small gully. The track leads gently up through the tall

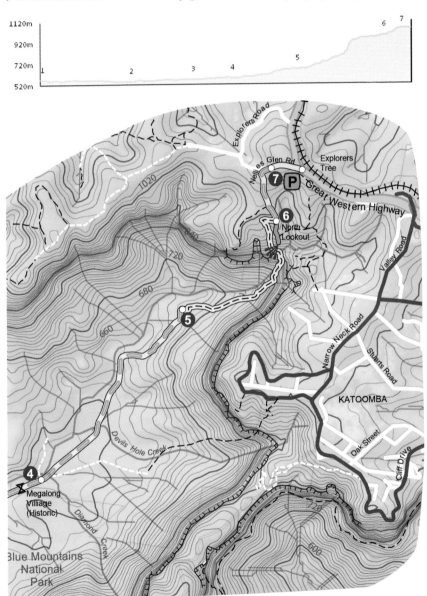

4 Megalong Valley to Explorers Tree

Point of interest – Megalong Village (Historic)

In 1870, kerosene shale was discovered in the area surrounding the upper end of Megalong and Diamond Creeks. In 1885, Mr J. B. North started to mine the resource, and the mine continued for nearly 10 years. During the life of the mine, the Megalong Village grew to a small town with a hotel, butchery, bakery, public hall and about 40 families. When the mines were closed in 1904, the best buildings were demolished and rebuilt in Katoomba. In December of 1904, a huge bushfire ripped up through the valley, destroying what buildings were left. This area is private land with a horse paddock with a view of the escarpment behind. A small bronze sign marks the site.

dense forest for about 700 metres, passing a *Nellies Glen* sign and a *Blue Mountains National Park* sign. The track continues fairly gently up along the side of the valley for another 400 metres before bending left and crossing below a small set of cascades. Walk up the steep Nellies Glen canyon steps for about 300 metres, passing alongside the tall

rock walls and crossing the usually small creek a few more times before passing through green timber chicanes. You'll find *Caution – Steep Descent* and *Pedestrian Access Only* signs at the top of this steep climb. Turn right and head up a widening trail for about 100 metres to pass a couple of *Nellies Glen* signs. Here the trail flattens out at an intersection marked

with a couple of *Six Foot Track* signs and a *Nellies Glen Bushland Restoration* sign.

6 Turn left, following the *Six Foot Track* sign uphill along the wide management trail. Continue up this trail, fairly steeply in places, for about 500 metres until the trail leads you around a locked metal gate. Here

Nellies Glen

4 Megalong Valley to Explorers Tree

Walk variation – Side Trip to Norths Lookout

From waypoint 6, turn right and walk through the gap in the large metal gate, over a small rise. The fairly narrow track soon leads down a series of timber steps, past some nice views, for just shy of 150 metres to pass a faint intersection with a track on your left, marked with a Bonnie Doon Fauna Study sign. Continue straight ahead, following the main track downhill for about 50 metres to the fenced and signposted Norths Lookout, with spectacular views over Nellies Glen and back into the valley you just walked out of. The lookout is named after John Britty North, also known as "the father of Katoomba" (1831-1917). North held large parcels of land in the area, and was involved in oil shale and coal mining, running several firms including the Katoomba Coal Mine. North was also engaged with his community by sitting on several boards and local council and was an active member of his local church. Return to waypoint 6 by retracing your steps back to the Six Foot Track, then continue straight ahead to complete the rest of the walk.

the trail flattens at a dirt car park with a shelter and the large *Six Foot Track* information sign.

7 Continue straight onto the sealed Nellies Glen Road and walk gently uphill and over the small rise following the road. After 200 metres, the road leads you past another small car parking area and comes to the Explorers Tree, just before the intersection with the Great Western Highway. Well done – you did it!

Walk variation – The 2.5 km walk extension to Katoomba train station

From the telegraph pole beside the dirt car park (near Explorers Tree), follow the tarmac footpath into the bush. This footpath leads over a small rise then zigzags downhill for a few hundred metres to beside the Great Western Highway. Veer right to step onto the concrete footpath, and follow this for 250 metres, then take the short detour along the side road (Bathurst Road) before rejoining the highway again. Keep following the footpath to the bus stop, then up the ramp, and turn right at Bathurst Road (also known as Main Street). Cross Narrow Neck Road, then cross Valley Road to follow Bathurst Road as it bends left. Now follow Bathurst Road for just shy of 1.5 kilometres, passing a few backpacker hostels, and crossing the roundabout at the pub. Once at the main shops, cross to the left side off Main Street, using the pedestrian crossing. The train station entrance is at the next roundabout opposite Katoomba Street.

Alternatively, you can avoid the highway altogether backtracking to waypoint 6 and following the Cliff Track which emerges at the end of Farnells Road. From here, you can pick your way through the backstreets of sleepy south Katoomba to get to the train station.

Point of interest – Explorers Tree, Katoomba

In 1813, the explorers Gregory Blaxland, William Wentworth and William Lawson, on their historic crossing of the Blue Mountains, engraved their names not only into the history books, but also reportedly into this tree on the side of Pulpit Hill. The tree, now long dead, was caged in 1884 in an attempt to preserve the engravings. The engravings are no longer visible and there has even been debate over the last 100 or so years as to the authenticity of the engravings.

Index

Notes